John Dennis, Aubrey De Vere

Poems

A Selection

John Dennis, Aubrey De Vere

Poems

A Selection

ISBN/EAN: 9783744713429

Printed in Europe, USA, Canada, Australia, Japan

Cover: Foto ©Thomas Meinert / pixelio.de

More available books at **www.hansebooks.com**

AUBREY DE VERE'S POEMS

A Selection.

EDITED BY

JOHN DENNIS,

AUTHOR OF "STUDIES IN ENGLISH LITERATURE," AND EDITOR OF
"ENGLISH SONNETS: A SELECTION."

CASSELL & COMPANY, LIMITED:

LONDON, PARIS & MELBOURNE.

1890.

CONTENTS.

	PAGE
PREFACE	vii

POEMS.

SONG—WHEN I WAS YOUNG	15
,, LOVE LAID DOWN	15
,, GIVE ME BACK MY HEART	16
,, MY HOPE IN HAPPIER DAYS ...	17
CHAUCER	17
THE SEARCH AFTER PROSERPINE ...	19
GREEK IDYLLS—I. GLAUCÈ	60
,, ,, II. IONÈ	62
,, ,, III. LYCIUS	65
ODE TO THE DAFFODIL	68
SONG—SOFTLY, O MIDNIGHT HOURS! ...	72
LOVE AND SORROW	73
DEATH IN CHILDBIRTH	75
THE DIGNITY OF SORROW	75
LOVE AND COUNSEL	77
ODE TO IRELAND	78
THE BARD ETHELL	82
THE WEDDING OF THE CLANS	94
UNA	96
FROM PSYCHE; OR, AN OLD POET'S LOVE ...	97
A SONG OF AGE	105
AGE	106
TO BURNS'S HIGHLAND MARY	106
ODE ON THE ASCENT OF THE ALPS ...	112
LINES WRITTEN UNDER DELPHI	123

SONNETS.

	PAGE
"Flowers I would Bring"	137
"She whom this Heart"	137
"The Happiest Lovers"	138
Incompatibility	139
Human Life	139
The Sun God	140
Urania	141
The Poetry of Life	141
Sorrow	142
National Apostasy	143
Universal History	143
Troilus and Cressida	144
"For We the Mighty Mountain Plains"	145
"Happy are They"	145
"The Spring of my Sweet Life"	146
I. Robert Browning	147
II. Robert Browning	147
A Winter Night in the Woods	148
I. Memorial	149
II. Memorial	149
III. Memorial	150

The Battle of Clontarf	151
The Three States of Womanhood	158
The Combat at the Ford	165
Scenes from 'Alexander the Great'	180
Cædmon the Cowherd	206
Bede's Last May	230
On Visiting a Haunt of Coleridge's	252
The Death of Copernicus	256
Autumnal Ode	273

PREFACE.

Mr. de Vere's poetry, like good wine, needs no bush ; but a few remarks by way of introducing this selection to the public may not be out of place.

Verse of a fine order is not necessarily popular. If it deal with large issues and does not appeal to momentary interests, if it be free from all attempts to catch the trick of the time, and expresses the nobler and more permanent aspects of human life, it will in all likelihood fail for a while to reach the position it can justly claim. A "fit audience" will, indeed, gladly listen to the poetic voice and appreciate its beauty ; but, invaluable though this judgment may be, since it indicates in a measure the verdict of futurity, it is not all-sufficing. A poet's hope is to touch the heart of his nation, even if— like Milton—he be content with a world so small and it is his joy to know that thoughts which have given pleasure to him are diffusing pleasure far and wide. This is surely an ambition which a man conscious of high powers may not unreasonably indulge.

It has been Mr. de Vere's object, as it was that of his great predecessor Wordsworth, not only to find his own reward in a career dedicated to poetry, but to dignify life as well as to adorn it. His aim is a high one, and is, therefore, not so readily understood, as if his mark were directed at a lower object. One of the most thoughtful poets of the age, it is possible that sometimes, though very rarely, his weight of matter may interfere with his art as a poet. The first object of poetry is to give delight, and it is only through the joy yielded by song that the poet can express his wisdom. If he fail to please as a singer, his efforts as a teacher will fail also. But the source of pleasure may lie deep, and a poet may demand much from his readers before he gives them the delight they crave. It is so with Mr. de Vere. Our love of his poetry is rarely love at first sight. His genius burns with a steady flame. He stands at the antipodes to the spasmodic poets once so popular, whose every page dazzled us, not indeed with fire from Heaven, but with sudden flashes as from a policeman's lantern.

Mr. de Vere makes no effort to allure the ears of the groundlings. "No poet of our day," it has been well said, "has done more to rouse his readers from petty and passing interests; no poet has struggled with nobler perseverance to make his readers look up towards the fountains of poetry."

Whether Mr. de Vere has been always happy in the choice of subjects, it is difficult to say—does not a poet make his subject as well as choose it? but it is not to be accounted strange that the legends which he relates with such admirable force and lucidity have in a measure failed to attract the public. The simplicity and directness of the epic are out of harmony with an age which prefers melodious verbiage to thought, and delights more in fantastical tricks of style than any period since the days of Donne and Cowley. To conceits of this kind no countenance has been given by Lord Tennyson, or by his friend Mr. de Vere, who while occupying a different and entirely original place in the spacious realm of poetry, resembles the Laureate in mastery of language, in vividness of perception, and in freedom from eccentricity.

I have been suggesting a reason why Mr. de Vere's poetry is not yet so widely known as one may hope it will some day be. Perhaps there is yet another. One of the signs of the times is pessimism, and another is a disregard of conscience. It has become a kind of fashion to extol the philosophy of Schopenhauer, who declared human life to be so wretched "that utter annihilation would be decidedly preferable;" and to praise Walt Whitman, with his rejection of moral responsibility, and his nakedness that knows no shame, as the great poet of the age. But Mr. de Vere is a Christian poet, and it is not necessary to accept all the dogmas of his Church—I for one am unable to do so—in order to appreciate the high standing he takes, and the faith and cheerful hope with which this Christian belief inspires his pages. His poetry appeals to us in our best moments, not through the direct instruction which is ever fatal to noble verse, but through the spirit that animates the whole.

All critics will admit that Mr. de Vere is a master of his instrument, and is capable of expressing a variety of harmonies. Each department of his verse is, I hope, illustrated in this Anthology. His sonnets may vie with the sweetest and subtlest sonnets of the century; his odes have the "pride and ample pinion" of a singer who on rising to his heaven of invention has left the earth far beneath him; his classic fancy has delightful play in the "Search after Proserpine," a comparatively early poem, while the influence of Greece is expressed in another but not less significant way in the "Lines written under Delphi."

Dramas written for the closet and not for the stage are somewhat of an anomaly, but the success of Sir Henry Taylor, and the achievement of Mr. de Vere's father, Sir Aubrey de Vere, whose "Mary Tudor" deserves far more recognition than it has received, may well have led the poet to make a similar venture. "Alexander the Great" is a noble drama, and it seems almost a sin to mutilate such a work of art by extracts. Yet I am unwilling to pass it by altogether, and I hope that the following passage from a review by one of the first critics of the day will suffice, if my selection fails, to show readers how worthy of their study is this highly poetical work.

After alluding to the difficulty of composing a drama, the scenes of which are always changing as the hero passes from country to country, the writer adds:—

"The apparent difficulty of the enterprise is, when surmounted, a measure of the skill and imaginative insight of the poet; and certainly in this case the enterprise appears to us to have been singularly successful. With hardly any of the common materials of dramatic interest, without any story of love that is not of the slightest kind, and absolutely subordinate to religious or political obligations, with nothing but the tale of heroic ambition for the chief subject of the tragedy, Mr. de Vere has yet not only rivetted our interest on his drama from the very beginning, but deepened that interest with every act and almost every scene to the truly tragic, and yet, in the truest sense, satisfying close."

Of Mr. de Vere's scope and charm as a writer of songs and lyrics, this volume may convey perhaps sufficient illustration. They will prove to some readers the most attractive part of the book, but apart from the odes and sonnets, I venture to think that there is no portion of the verse illustrated, more characteristic of the poet's genius, which is both deeply reflective and vividly imaginative, than such poems as "Cædmon the Cowherd," "The Death of Copernicus," and

"Bede's Last May." "The Legends of St. Patrick" having been already published in Messrs. Cassell's National Library it has been thought well to select nothing from a poem produced in so popular a form, but this need not hinder me saying that some of the poet's most characteristic verse is to be found in that little volume. The poem consists of fifteen legends, "The Striving of St. Patrick on Mount Cruachan" being perhaps the most striking.

Nothing more remains to be said, since this is not the place for an elaborate criticism of Mr. de Vere's poetry. All I have wished to do in these introductory remarks is to point out to readers at present ignorant of the poet's work a few of its prominent features.

J. D.

IN A FEW POEMS OMISSIONS HAVE BEEN MADE WITH THE AUTHOR'S APPROVAL.

Aubrey de Vere's Poems.
A Selection.

POEMS.

SONG.

When I was young, I said to Sorrow
  'Come, and I will play with thee :'—
He is near me now all day,
And at night returns to say,
'I will come again to-morrow,
  I will come and stay with thee.'

Through the woods we walk together ;
  His soft footsteps rustle nigh me ;
To shield an unregarded head
He hath built a winter shed ;
And all night long in rainy weather,
  I hear his gentle breathings by me.

SONG.

Love laid down his golden head
  On his mother's knee ;
'The world runs round so fast,' he said,
  'None has time for me.'

Thought, a sage unhonoured, turned
    From the on-rushing crew ;
Song her starry legend spurned ;
    Art her glass down threw.

Roll on, blind world, upon thy track
    Until thy wheels catch fire !
But that is gone which comes not back
    To seller nor to buyer !

SONG.

Give me back my heart, fair child ;
    To you as yet 'twere worth but little ;
Half beguiler, half beguiled,
    Be you warned, your own is brittle.

' Hid it ! dropt it on the moors !
    ' Lost it and you cannot find it '—
My own heart I want, not yours :
    You have bound and must unbind it.

Fling it from you ; youth is strong ;
    Love is trouble, love is folly ;
Love, that makes an old heart young
    Makes a young heart melancholy.

SONG.

My hope, in happier days than these;
    My love—hope past;
Memory's one star on lonely seas;
    My anchor, last!
Why ask'st thou with subdued surprise
    And that mild glee
Wherefore I turn, still turn mine eyes
    From all, to thee?

The blind man turns—and none forbids—
    Into sunshine
His filmy, cold, unlighted lids:
    The deaf incline
Toward harps whence songs for them unborn
    Float, light and free;
To graves long cherished, hearts forlorn!
    And I to thee.

CHAUCER.

Escaped from the city, its smoke, its glare,
    'Tis pleasant, showers over and birds in chorus,
To sit in green alleys and breathe cool air
    Which the violet only has breathed before us!

Such healthful solace is ours, forsaking
   The glass-growth of modern and modish rhyme
For the music of days when the Muse was breaking
   On Chaucer's pleasance like dawn's sweet prime.

Hands rubbed together smell still of earth;
   The hot-bed verse has a hot-bed taint;
'Tis sense turned sour, its cynical mirth;
   'Tis pride, its darkness; its blush, 'tis paint.

His song was a feast where thought and jest
   Like monk and franklin alike found place;
Good Will's Round Table! There sat as guest
   Shakesperean insight with Spenser's grace.

His England lay laughing in Faith's bright morn!
   Life in his eye looked as rosy and round
As the cheek of the huntsman that blows on the horn
   When the stag leaps up and loud bays the hound.

King Edward's tourney, fair Blanche's court,
   Their clarions, their lutes in his verse live on;
But he loved better the birds' consort
   Under oaks of Woodstock while rose the sun.

The cloister, the war-field tented and brave,
   The shout of the burghers in hostel or hall,
The embassy grave over ocean's wave,
   And Petrarch's converse—he loved them all.

In Spring, when the breast of the lime-grove
    gathers
  Its roseate cloud; when the flushed streams
    sing,
And the mavis tricks her in gayer feathers,
  Read Chaucer then; for Chaucer is Spring!

On lonely evenings in dull Novembers,
  When rills run choked under skies of lead,
And on forest-hearths the year's last embers,
  Wind-heaped and glowing, lie, yellow and red,

Read Chaucer still! In his ivied beaker
  With knights and wood-gods and saints embossed,
Spring hides her head till the wintry breaker
  Thunders no more on the far-off coast.

THE SEARCH AFTER PROSERPINE.

OF all the beautiful fictions of Greek Mythology there are few more exquisite than the story of Proserpine, and none deeper in symbolical meaning. Considering the fable with reference to the physical world, Bacon says, in his "Wisdom of the Ancients," that by the Rape of Proserpine is signified the disappearance of flowers at the end of the year, when the vital juices are, as it were, drawn down to the central darkness and held there in bondage. The fable has, however, its moral significance also, being connected with that great mystery of Joy and Grief, of Life and Death, which pressed so heavily on the mind of Pagan Greece, and imparts to the whole of her mythology a profound interest, spiritual as well as philosophical.

SCENE I.

IN SICILY.

Ceres, Fountain Nymphs.

CERES.

I.

Through every region I have sought her ;
  Each shore has answered back my moan :
  As Summer slides from zone to zone
  Winding Earth's beauty in his own
Thus, seeking thee, my long lost daughter,
  I wander ever, sad and lone.
  Empty in Heaven my throne remains ;
  Unblest expand my harvest plains.

II.

I've searched the deep Sicilian meads,
  And sacred Latium, where of yore
  Saturn hid his forehead hoar ;
I've sought her by the Alphean reeds ;
  Where solitary Cyclops squanders
  On the unlistening oleanders
Vain song that makes the sea-wells quiver
I've sought my child, and seek for ever.

III.

By Cretan lawns and vales oak-sprinkled,
By sands of Libya, brown and wrinkled,
And where for leagues, o'er Nile, is borne
The murmur of the yellowing corn,
And where o'er Ida's sea-like plain
White, waving harvests mock the main ;
Past Taurus, and past Caucasus,
Have I been vainly wandering thus ;
 In vain the Heavens my absence mourn,
And Iris' self in vain is faint
With wafting down their old complaint ;
 O'er earth, unresting though outworn,
 I roam for aye a shape forlorn.
Hark, hark they sing—

FOUNTAIN NYMPHS.

I.

Proserpina was playing
 In the soft Sicilian clime,
'Mid a thousand damsels maying
 All budding to their prime :
From their regions azure-blazing
The Immortal Concourse gazing
Bent down and sought in vain
Another shape of earth so meet with them to
 reign.

II.

The steep blue arch above her
  In Jove's own smiles arrayed
Shone mild, and seemed to love her:
  His steeds Apollo stayed:
Soon as the God espied her
Nought else he saw beside her,
  Though in that happy clime
A thousand maids were verging to the fulness of
    their prime.

III.

Old venerable Ocean
  Against the meads uprolled
With ever-young emotion
  His tides of blue and gold:
He had called with pomp and pæan
From his well-beloved Ægean
  All billows to one shore,
To fawn around her footsteps and in murmurs to
    adore.

IV.

Proserpina was playing
  Sicilian flowers among;
Amid the tall flowers straying:
  Alas! she strayed too long!

Sometimes she bent and kissed them,
Sometimes her hands caressed them,
 And sometimes, one by one,
She gathered them and tenderly enclosed them in
 her zone.

   Lay upon your lips your fingers—
    Ceres comes, and full of woe ;
   Sad she comes, and often lingers ;
    Well that grief divine I know :
   Lay upon your lips your fingers ;
   Crush not as you run the grass ;
   Let the little bells of glass
    On the fountain blinking
   Burst, but ring not till she pass,
    Down in silence sinking.
   By the green scarf arching o'er her,
    By her mantle yellow-pale,
   By those blue weeds bent before her,
    Bent as in a gale,
   Well I know her—hush, descend—
   Hither her green-tracked footsteps wend.

CERES.

Fair nymphs ! whose music o'er the meadows
   gliding
Hath been your gentle herald, and for me
A guide obsequious to this spot—fair nymphs !

Fair graceful nymphs, my daughter's sweet companions,
Say, say but where she dwells; claiming from me,
In turn, what boon you will.

NYMPHS.

Alas, we know not!

CERES.

May the pure ripple of your founts for ever
Leap up, unsoiled, against their verdurous banks;
May your fresh kisses ripple up as lightly,
As softly, and with undiscovering noise,
Against the embowering arms of prisoning lovers,
Shadowing the charms they seek!

NYMPHS.

We have no lovers.

CERES.

No, and need none. Alas, Proserpina,
Thou wert as these! so innocent no fountain,
Nor half so gay; no flower so light, so fair.
Ah, fair mild Nymphs, my daughter's sweet companions!
May Jove, as ye run by, make blind the eyes
Of Wood-gods and the Fauns; in matted ivy
Tangle their beards; catch them in sudden clefts

Of deep-mossed stems, till ye have glided by—
But tell me where she dwells.

NYMPHS.

Goddess ! we know not.

CERES.

Tell me then how ye lost her

NYMPHS.

We were playing
After our caverned sleep which the high Gods
Sent us while Phœbus flamed too near the earth,
We played like summer bees involved and sang ;
Some combing pearls from sandy slopes, some blowing
In shells, or lily-tubes our watery conchs ;
When suddenly rolled forth long peals of thunder
Far, far below. Earth shook ; trembling we sank
Into our beds, amazed : when up we floated
A divine darkness hovered o'er the earth,
And from that moment we have had no flowers ;
No flower since then in flower-famed Sicily !
And we no more behold Proserpina
That played with us so sweetly. We have made
A melody that tells of her and sing it
Lest we should grieve.

CERES.

     Yes, I have heard your song:
Still the same tale—the words themselves unchanged—
Know you no more?

NYMPHS.

     Goddess, not wide our knowledge!
Phœbus cares nought for Nymphs, lonely flower-bathers;
Nor other prophet see we. Yet of late
Our vales are flushed with new strange visitants;
Their tumult ofttimes as the sun descends
Shakes us within our lily-paved pavilions;
And when we look abroad along the marge
The inland vales, shaggy with pine and ilex,
That catch like nets those boy-nymphs, the light Zephyrs,
Are filled with riot. From all sides they rush
Mad Gods, with russet brows the west outfacing,
And wands tossed high; in song the lawns are drowned.
Help us, great Jove! Fair Goddess, once it chanced
As this red festival came reeling by,
Over the fount in which trembling we lay
Some Wood-god crushed a wreath of poisonous berries

Laughing; and our bright home all crimson grew,
So that we wept. I pray you, gentle Goddess,
Protect us from these Gods.

CERES.

Ha! Bacchus here!
I thought my little late-born enemy
Lay hid in Hellas. What, and merry grown,
With revellers! then haply he hath stolen
My beauteous child. Mild nymphs, my child's
   companions!
Mild, silver-footed nymphs with silver songs!
Where dwell those Wood-gods when they come
   not hither?

NYMPHS.

At Naxos, Fame reports; an unblessed isle.

CERES.

Farewell, sweet nymphs; from them, and from all
   perils
May Jove defend you well! I seek those Gods,
And I will pray them that they hurt you not.

NYMPHS.

First Semichorus.
Without aid of plumes
   Light-footing the sea brine,
The dimness she illumes
   Of evening's gray decline;

The wild streams, proud to waft her,
    In dappled purple glide,
With a shadowed green track after,
    And a sunny green beside.

Second Semichorus.
Down, nymphs, into the waters!
    The air is rough with sighs,
The earth is red with slaughters;
    Down, down, and seldom rise!
Our crystal dome above us,
    And the star-dome yet more high,
Nor care nor pain can move us
    Whilst here we laugh and lie!

SCENE II.
NAXOS.
Ceres, Wood-gods.

CERES.

A Bacchic wood! the pine stems and old oaks
Are swathed with crimson under their green
    shadows!
A wilderness of wood! within its ambush
Armies of men might lurk. Above the trees
A gloom voluptuous undulates and hovers
Like a dark fleece of wine-dewed gossamer.
The caverns, as I pass them, mildly breathe

A colder current of wine-scented air
Into my face. Ha, ha,—a tiger's roar!
And now a din of resonant wild laughter
That makes the forest like a reed-pipe ring.
The very beasts have caught the infectious madness,
And ramp with sport irreverent on high Gods.
Down, leopard, down—ha, myriad-moonèd panther,
Away! 'tis well for you this almond branch
Is sheathed in flowers Sicilia feeds no longer;
That cry had else been louder. Hark, they come!

FAUNS AND WOOD-GODS.

First Strophe.

Lift, lift the vine-wreathed goblet up,
    Where lies the fierce wine darkling;
Now Bacchus leaps from out the cup:
    See, see his black eyes sparkling!
Hark, how the bubbles upward throw
    A low song and soft coiling;
'Tis Bacchus' self that laughs below,
    To keep his red fount boiling!

First Antistrophe.

Great Bacchus with his conquering hands
    Upraised the far-sought treasure
Of all the oceans, all the lands
    Afloat in one wild pleasure.

Lo ! how it plunges, rolls, and sweeps !
  Great Bacchus bathes beneath it ;
What odour from the eddy leaps !
  Great Bacchus' self doth breathe it.

Second Strophe.

Through us he rises from the ground ;
  These sharp-leaved chaplets draw him
Into our tresses ivy-crowned :
  In purple flames I saw him !
Lift every thyrsus high and higher ;
  While round and round ye wind them
Great Bacchus turns the air to fire,
  Wide crowns of fire behind them !

Second Antistrophe.

Drink, drink to Bacchus, every limb
  With wine will soon be glowing :
He drinks to those that drink to him,
  Himself on all bestowing.
Into the hearts of all his wards
  He pours, like streams from Pindus,
The strength and speed of all the pards
  That rolled his car by Indus !

CERES.

O Fauns and Satyrs of the merry forests !
Sharp-hoofed, long-horned, nymph-dreaded deities !

Grant me this hour your aid. Secrets I know
Of herbs grass-hidden and medicinal blossoms
Whereof one leaf, into your cups distilled,
Would make them rise into a fount of foam
Wide as the broad arch of yon flowering myrtle:
Those secrets shall be yours—only restore me
My infant child.

FAUNS.

O venerable Goddess!
Large-browed, large-eyed, presence august and
    holy!
In our green forests dwells no infant child.

CERES.

But she is now in truth no infant child
As when I laid her 'mid the sacred flowers
Of Sicily, with Nymphs for her young nurses
And tender playmates.

FAUNS.

Venerable Goddess!
No child have we beheld, nor ever shall,
With mien like thine.

CERES.

Ah! she was not like me!
I was her mother; but like her no more

Than the dark ground is like some flower, star-
    bright,
That from it springs, and o'er it waves in beauty.

FAUNS.

In Sicily you lost her?

CERES.

     Wood-gods, yes.

FIRST FAUN.

And I remember now in that soft isle
Such creature we beheld as you have lost.
Upon a vernal bank she sat alone
Among the aërial mounds and honeyed meadows;
Wearied she seemed, yet smiled in weariness,
And, as a garden, was with bright flowers crowned;
Many she held upon her lap, and many
Fell down about her feet; her feet gleamed through
    them.
Strange fear, albeit to fear unused, we felt;
And, beckoning to each other, slow retired.
Since then in vain we seek her.

CERES.

       Woodland Gods!
Was she not fair?

SECOND FAUN.

    So fair that on the earth
Is left no longer any shape of beauty.

Well spake you, calling her your infant child.
Such light was on her brow—within her eyes
Such gleam immediate of celestial gladness
A child she seemed, by that inspiring clime
Divinely ripened in one summer day
To full perfection of virginal beauty.
Not far the playmate nymphs their wild hymns
    sang,
Like birds new-touched by the enamouring season :
While we went back dreading the wrath of Jove.

CERES.

Since she is lost those songs are heard no more.
In vain the sea-worn mariners suspend
Long time their oars amid the drifting spray ;
In vain the home-bound shepherds pause and
    listen ;
Nor any flower is seen.

FAUNS.

          Maternal Goddess!
Still in one spot lingers a wreath of flowers.

CERES.

'Tis strange—those flowers, where are they ?

FAUNS.

              At the entrance
Of a long glen, that sinks in dimness down
From the proud pastures arched along the sea.

CERES.

Ha, Woodland Gods! that was her place of play;
A haunt unknown to men.

FAUNS.

Hark, hark, 'tis Bacchus!

CERES.

But tell me, Gods—

FAUNS.

We thirst, we thirst for wine;
Give, give us wine, and we will stay with you;
Roll it in deep floods forth from cleft and cavern.

CERES.

Stay, Wood-gods, stay!

FAUNS.

Ha, ha, that laugh; 'tis Bacchus!
(*They rush past singing.*)

First Strophe.

Hour by hour the vines are growing
    Over pine and over rock;
The blood, like fire within them flowing,
    With bounding pulse and merry shock
Each green spray uplifts and pushes
Till the loftiest ridge it brushes.

First Antistrophe.

Hour by hour great Bacchus nurses
 The wide wreaths of his anadem ;
In him they meet, and he disperses
 Himself o'er all the world in them.
The mountains of all seas and lands,
He grasps them in his thousand hands.

Second Strophe.

The gums from yonder pine-bough dropping
 Like fire-lit jewels darkly shine ;
The ivy-wreaths yon goat is cropping
 Are drenched in mist of purple wine :
The Vine, a honey-venomed snake,
Hath bit and swollen each brier and brake.

Second Antistrophe.

The forest burgeons giant-flowers
 As on this generous food it feeds ;
Warming its roots in crimson showers
 That bead the earth with Bacchic seeds :
A sacred wood : his house of mirth
The God that conquers all the earth !

Epode.

The carpets of these halls of joyaunce
 Uplift us with so fierce a spring,
That we, to balance that upbuoyaunce,
 Deep draught on draught are forced to fling.

Hark, hark, his laugh! we cannot stay;
Blue skies, farewell! away, away!

CERES.

To Sicily once more. Lo! how these vines
Have grown about me! never infant yet
Tangled like this young Bacchus his embraces;
Not one upon the earth! another year
And half my kingdom he'll have won from me
As Hermes robbed Apollo of his herd.
No feastful, sunlit mound, or yellow hill,
Will sing, at evening, anthems unto me;
No shelving corn-field on the mountain-slope
Make westering Phœbus, while askance he peers
Down through the pale stems, green with jealousy.
Parnassian weed, away! ah, lost Proserpina!
Thou, thou wert as my flowers—unsought for mine,
And then, once mine, more dear than all my
　　wealth!
The Gods in their Olympian mansions know
Nothing of grief: children they too have lost;
But never mourned as I have. Surely I
Have caught from Earth some portion of her
　　sadness,
And heart maternal of Humanity.
To Sicily once more. O fair Sicilia!
Those flowers they saw, whence came they and
　　what mean they?

That must my search discover; I must see them;
When I behold them I shall see once more
What I in vain desire—my child's fair eyes.
Down, vine-wreaths, down! I break from you away.

SCENE III.

SICILIAN SEA.

(*Nereids sing.*)

Strophe.

Far off the storms were dying;
   The Sea-nymphs and Sea-gods
On new-lulled billows lying,
   With tridents and pearl-rods,
Upon their sliding thrones
   And beds of waving waters
Reclined august, old Ocean's sons
   And the choir of his foam-white daughters.

Antistrophe.

Into their deep conchs blowing
   They smoothed the scowling waves,
And the great sea-music forth flowing
   Was echoed in the glassy caves.
There was no sound but song
   Save now and then far under,
When an ocean monster streamed along
   With a roll of Ocean's thunder.

Epode.

Then Iris, lightly dropping,
   Leaped from her cloudy screen,
And lit on a wave down-sloping
   In floods of crimson-green :
A moment its neck she trod,
   And cried, 'The Gods of Heaven
'Are coming to feast with the Ocean-god,
'So Jove has sworn, this even.'

GLAUCÈ.

Fair Sisters, ocean-cradled, wave-revered !
Holds not this evening well the morning's pledge ?
Salt gust no more ; nor airy arc, down-showering
Into the dim green, rain of sunny gems
Or crowns celestial ; crystal chasm no more
By harsh winds crushed to murmuring foam
    abysses ;
But, wide o'er all a plenitude of light
Serene as that which sits on Jove's great brow ;
And breeze as equable as Juno's breath.

AUTONOE.

And, Sisters, mark ! along yon opal Heaven
And sea of agate and chalcedony
The promised pageant spreads. We shall behold
The mighty head of Jove, rich-tressed, supreme,
Sacred and strong and fair and venerable,

With golden sceptre and obedient eagle :
And we shall gaze on Juno's large mild eyes,
And the sea-born Queen of Beauty, her who runs
Over the swelling hearts of Gods and men
As Thetis glides over the ocean waves;
And, dearer still to us, the graceful form
Of Hebe, solitary nymph of Heaven,
Alone among the Gods and yet not lonely.
Thus Iris spake.

EUDORA.

      Fair Iris! dropped she then
This morn from Heaven, her ocean spoils to gather?
I knew it not, for on the Libyan sands
All day I rolled a great smooth shell, too great
To clasp or carry : but my tears are past,
Since we shall gaze upon high Gods.

GLAUCÈ.

         Lo, there!
How the red west inflames the deep! Methinks
That merry God, conqueror of many a land,
His banners over ocean too is waving;
To Britain will he drive us, end of earth?
See, I have dropped my bracelet.

AUTONOE.

        Over ocean
That God advances; dark-rimmed Naxian shores

Already with his tendril nets are swathed,
Yea and the Naxian billows ; all day long
We toss them backward from our foam-white
    bosoms,
And beds of billows, to their beds of sand.

EUDORA.

And maids of earth he mocks at worse than us :
Last evè, by yonder meadow I was floating,
Pillowing my cheek upon a sleepy wave
And harkening to an inland pipe remote
When suddenly the purpled shore resounded
With tumult harsh ; and concourse I beheld
Of Wood-gods on the sands, leaping and laugh-
    ing;
And why ? because a gentle maid of earth
That with her mortal playmate had been straying
Beneath the bank, oppressed perhaps with sleep,
(Who knows ? I know not), when she thought not
    of it,
In vine-nets prisoned lay : The Wood-gods
    mocked !
Bacchus such puissance hath—

GLAUCÈ.

                How wretched those
That dwell on Earth ! alas, I pity them !
On that rough, heavy element opaque

What lovely light can glimmer ? None can tell
Wherefore the high Gods shaped the hump-backed
   Earth !

EUDORA.

Nay, Sister, when the forests slant as now
From the ridged mountains to the wine-black
   sea,
And Phœbus on their gold and vermeil roof
Looks brightly, while the winds rush under them,
Then hath the Earth her beauty—yea, a gleam
Like our Autonoe, when her sun-loved tresses
Upon a green rock loosening she flings forth,
Laughing, into some monster's briny eyes.

AUTONOE.

You speak well, Sister, courteous like the Gods;
And blossoming fruit-trees, spangled with sea
   spray,
Are fair indeed at sunrise : Earth hath gleams
As Nubian slaves their gems; yet how forlorn
And like a slave's her downcast countenance !
Her hues are not like ocean's, coloured lights,
But coloured shades ; dim shadows painted o'er ;
Yea and the motions of her trees and harvests
Resemble those of slaves, reluctant, slow,
By outward force compelled; not like our billows,
Springing elastic in impetuous joy,
Or indolently swayed.

EUDORA.

Not less o'erawed
Are those that dwell on Earth, harsh-speaking
    Mortals.
One eve, it chanced, into a glen I wandered,
In garb a boy: unwonted weight I felt;
The shades moved not; dull odours thronged the
    air;
Up from the ground a dense, blunt sound was
    rushing;
All creatures ranged as though beneath their feet
Down to Earth's centre chains unseen were hung,
And languid browsed as from necessity
Not joy, their faint sighs leaving on the grass.
All things were sad; sadly I wandered on
To where there lay a something large and black,
And panting; some Immortal deeming it,
With reverence I was passing, when, behold!
Hard by there stood a company of Mortals,
Wailing; and myrrh on myrrh, and oil on oil,
O'er it in grief they flung; it was a pyre:
Homeward I turned abashed, and weeping much
For Man's unhappy race, so fair yet sad,
By Jove's great wrath oppressed and shame of
    death;
Yes, and weep still; for know you, gentle Sisters,
Though Gods themselves should dwell upon the
    Earth,

Grief they must feel; the affliction men call love,
Or hunger, or the grave.

AUTONOE.

Down, Sisters, down!
In sorrow footing the bright ocean-way
I see that form half human, all divine:
'Tis Ceres; plunge we down! No nymph she loves
Save her child's mates.

GLAUCÈ.

Yea, and of those is jealous

SCENE IV.

THE SICILIAN SHORE.

Ceres, Fountain Nymphs.

CERES.

Inconstant waves, farewell: I love you not:
Earth, I salute thee, fruitful, though in sorrow.
Still on! my search, though vain, is all my rest.
One flower of hers, to this sad bosom folded,
Will give it back its old Olympian calm.
The nymphs sing low: O for thy songs, Proserpina,
That woke the ice-bound streams, while old boughs leaped
Though dead, into the glory of fresh blossoms!

(*Fountain Nymphs sing.*)

I.

Proserpina was lying
  Against her ebon throne;
Alternating long sighing
  With a shudder and a moan:
The dull Lethean river
  Whose breath the nightshade breeds
Went toiling on for ever
  Through the forest of its reeds:
    'O mother, I was playing
      ''Mid the soft Sicilian air—
    'For ever must I languish
      'In this empire of Despair!'

II.

With wide and sable gleaming
  In chains decreed of old
Through grey morasses streaming
  That ancient river rolled:
The hemlock borders under
  Drave the voluminous flood,
With a low, soft, sleepy thunder
  That thrilled the stagnant blood:
    'O mother, I was playing
      ''Mid the soft Sicilian air—
    'For ever must I languish
      'In this empire of Despair!'

III.

No bird was there to warble,
  The wind was void of sound ;
Vast caves of jet-black marble
  Were yawning all around ;
No placid Heaven, blue-tented,
  Its dome above her spread ;
Like clouds the Souls tormented
  Were drifting overhead :
    'O mother, I was playing
      ''Mid the soft Sicilian air—
    'For ever must I languish
      'In this empire of Despair ! '

IV.

Darkness but faintly chequered
  Possessed that region dim,
Save one white cloud that flickered
  Above the horizon's rim ;
Under the dreary lustre
  It cast in flakes and showers
Up rose afar the cluster
  Of Pluto's palace towers :
    'O mother, I was playing
      ''Mid the soft Sicilian air—
    'For ever must I languish
      'In this empire of Despair ! "

V.

Proserpina for ever
  Thereon her large eyes kept
While gusts from that cold river
  Her tresses backward swept;
Ever in sadness lying
  Against her ebon throne,
With her melancholy sighing
  Half smothered in a moan:
   'O mother, I was playing
    ''Mid the soft Sicilian air—
   'Must I languish here for ever
    'In this empire of Despair?'

CERES.

O Nymphs, where found you that despondent
    song?
And why this funeral chime? She is immortal.

NYMPHS.

Immortal truly, venerable Goddess!
And yet in Erebus she dwells; and plays
No more; no flowers to play with finds she there.

CERES.

How know you this?

NYMPHS.

          Last eve we wandered forth
By fugitive rainbows lured and rain-washed grass

To that deep valley where we lost our playmate ;
And for the first time past it. In one spot
We found, with joy astonished, crowds of flowers ;
Flowers of all kinds, each larger than its kind,
And brighter : wandering here and there among
    them,
Behold two mighty chariot tracks ! deep fissures,
Burning and black, to where the opposing bank
Locked in and barred the vale : the rocks were
    split ;
Dull vapours hovering o'er them. In a moment
The truth flashed on us, and we heard, yea felt
Once more, that subterraneous thunder roll.
The King of Darkness, Monarch sole below,
Looked up and saw thy child, and thirsted for
    her ;
And snatched her to his shades :—In Erebus
Thy daughter dwells.

CERES.

No song, no fable this !
Ah flower ! pure lily among the unfruitful shades
White lonely lamp of all the Elysian darkness !
Ah child ! the daughter of an unblest fate,
Thou hast no mother now : thou hast forgotten
That e'er thou hadst a mother—Woe, woe, woe !
The imperial diadem doth mock that brow,
The sceptre doth subdue that little hand

More than the Shades, thy subjects! Gentle nymphs,
Let me behold that spot.

FIRST NYMPH.

         With slow, sad foot
—On grey autumnal eves, the Nymphs themselves
With slow, sad foot, o'er the dim grass steal on—
Advance! no bounding step, fair sister Nymphs;
No bounding step, or jubilant, reckless song.
Lo, there the gleam! a breeze, a sigh divine
Is ever sweeping o'er those tremulous flowers,
Troubling their dews that fall not, held, like tears
In melancholy eyes—O fair, fair flowers!
Ye, as she dropped you, instantly took root,
And fade not ever. Immortality
Ye caught from the last pressure of those hands;
Immortal were ye though the world should die.

NYMPHS.

First Semichorus.

Looks divine, divinely chastened,
 Sad eyes, on the saddened ground
As by spells eternal fastened,
 Folded hands, and locks unbound!
Deeper, every moment deeper,
 Pierce those eyes her daughter's shroud;
The earth to this immortal weeper
 Grows half transparent as a cloud;

And her ears even now are ringing
With old Lethe's mournful singing.

Second Semichorus.

But see, on high the blue is riven !
That radiance ! Hermes it must be !
Around him smiles the flattered Heaven ;
  No Apollonian flight hath he
Right onward, nor the stormy wrath
  Of Jove's great Eagle earthward rushing,
But winds along in serpent path
  Through maiden airs around him flushing
With wingèd feet and rod upholden,
Enwreathed with mild Persuasions golden.

HERMES.

Hermes, mild herald of the Gods, I come,
Bearing the grace of Jove, upon my lips
Distilled—high kiss of heavenly benediction.
Goddess to Mortals and Immortals dear,
Be of good cheer : Proserpina, beloved
Of all the blest Olympians, sceptred sits
In Tartarus ; sole bride of him that sways
The world heroic of Departed Souls ;
A child although a Queen ; and, though a spouse,
Yet virgin ever ; tempering the deep heart
Of Pluto, and to all the Shades as dear
As Dian to the night, or to the waves

The foam-dividing star of Aphrodite.
Sacred and well beloved—a Mystery—
Fares she not well? Maternal Goddess! raise
The large dejected orbs of thy fair eyes,
And gaze on him upon whose brow doth meet
The light of all the Gods giving command:
Look up and speak!

CERES.

Mild herald Mercury!
Thy voice is in mine ears; wingèd and sweet
Ever its tones; brightening all hearts, like Heaven
When Jove looks up: but now, unwonted softness
Melts through their pauses. Dost thou pity me?
Then herald God, auspicious guide of Shades,
Mighty art thou in the Unbeloved Abode;
Restore, restore my child!

HERMES.

Not comfort only,
Deep-bosomed Goddess, grave, and dulcet-voiced,
But aid I bear: and need there is of both.
Alone she sits beyond the utmost bound
Of laughter from the Gods, or shaft Phœbean,
And thou art justly restless for thine own.
Hear then the ordinance of Jove; descend!
Yon rock shall like a billow arch thy way;
Descend into the Stygian waste; behold
Once more thy tender daughter face to face;

Kiss her once more, once more upon thy knee
And in thine arms possess her. This is much :
Yet more : if seed not yet of flower or fruit
Unblessed have touched her lips, henceforth and
    ever
With thee she dwells in sweet society.
Descend ! the Will of Jove before thee running
Makes smooth thy path, and the Caducean charm
Waved from this wand, around thy feet shall
    beckon   .
A quire of bright Immortals fit to grace
The steps of a departing Deity.
Ethereal Seasons ! from the snowy clouds
Your ambient nests on cold autumnal days
Hover once more about this spot ; and ye
Gift-feathered Hours at Heaven's wide gate for
    ever
On broad and billowy wing suspense, the cord
Aërial, that detains you bursting fly
With unreverting faces to the earth,
And breathe a sudden spring on valley and plain :
And ye, infantine Zephyrs, on whose lips
The Gods have breathed ; thou too, delight of
    Heaven,
Iris ! descend ; and o'er the shadowy glen
Thy many coloured scarf from both thy hands
Fling wide, and cast the brightest of thy smiles
Upon the head of this descending Power.

FIRST NYMPH.

Behold! into the chasm she walks.

SECOND NYMPH.

But lo!
How rich a splendour burns on yonder bank!
The trees grow lustrous as Apollo's locks;
Between the arch of yon suspended bow
And the green hollow, flows a low deep music,
With light songs o'er it playing in wantonness;
Hark, hark, once more.

(*The Hours Sing.*)
Strophe.

A beam on Earth's chill bosom
    Falls pointed 'mid her sleep;
And leaf and bud and blossom
    Up from their dull trance leap;
That beam at Earth's dim centre
Hath found the mailèd Winter,
    And touched his snow-cold lips;
Upon his breast that beam doth rest
    And frost-bound finger tips.

Antistrophe.

From deep grass gently heaving
    Quick flowers in myriads rise,
A wreath for Winter weaving;
    It falls below his eyes;

His old grey beard it covers
Like locks of mirthful lovers;
  It makes him laugh with pride,
As he a youth had grown in sooth
  And found a youthful Bride.

(*The Zephyrs sing.*)
Strophe.

The bright-lipped waters troubling
  Of the cold Olympian springs,
We caught the airs up-bubbling
  And stayed them with our wings;
From the beginning sealed
Like sweet thoughts unrevealed
  Those airs till then lay hid;
Like odours barred in buds yet hard
  Or the eye beneath the lid.

Antistrophe.

Our pinions mildly swaying
  With an undulating grace
We bid those airs go playing
  Over Earth's beaming face;
On the laurel banks new-flowered,
On the ridge of pine dew-showered,
  On every leaf and blade
That leaps on wings and all but sings
  In sunshine or in shade!

(Hours and Zephyrs sing together.)
Strophe.
Over the olives hovering,
  Brushing the myrtle bowers,
Dark ground with blossoms covering
  The Zephyrs and the Hours
With laugh and gentle mocking
We play, the green boughs rocking,
  Above each other rolled
From laurel leaf to laurel leaf
  That sing like tongues of gold !

Antistrophe.
Now like birds fast flitting
  On from bough to bough,
Like bees in sunshine knitting
  Murmuring mazes now ;
    Parting oft—oft blending,
    And for ever sending
Spangled showers around,
With eddying streams of scents and gleams,
And deep Olympian sound.

(Sicilian Nymphs singing.)
First Strophe.
Numbers softer than our own
  And in happier circle running
Like Flora's crown or Venus' zone
  They are braiding in their cunning.

All the God-thronged air is glowing
  With a ferment of delight,
All the flowers in rapture blowing
  Every moment swell more bright
And higher round the pale stems clamber
In vermilion wreaths or amber.

First Antistrophe.

Half in terror, half in pleasure,
  Little birds on warm boughs waking
Launch abroad a rival measure,
  Floral births with songs o'ertaking :
O'er the shadows little lights
  And o'er little lights a shadow
Bound along like gamesome sprites
  On the green waves of the meadow ;
And new streams are up and boiling,
And new insects round them coiling.

Second Strophe.

On one side a cedarn alley,
  On the other a myrrh brake,
Downward streams the mystic valley
  As flushed rivers their path take
By hills their devious waters curbing ;
  Airs ambrosial forth are swung
From boughs their crimson fruitage orbing ;
  Iris, borne those airs among

Flings o'er the dim wildernesses
Her illumed dishevelled tresses.

Second Antistrophe.

Through a mist of sunny rays
   Gleam bright eyes and pinions shiver;
O'er the mountain's breast of bays
   Panting dew-gems bask and quiver;
All the Gods with silent greeting
   In this sumptuous harbour met
Make the palace of their meeting
   Rich as Juno's cabinet,
Golden-domed and golden-gated,
With sacred pleasures never sated.

Hush—wild song, no more!
   Nor dance of lyric lightness—
A shadow from the shore
   Steals and blots the brightness.
   Like children tired of play
   The splendours melt away:
Trips by each elf—mark! Iris' self
   Dissolves in waning whiteness.

IRIS.

I have but leaped from out my airy lustres
To plant my white foot palpably on Earth.
Fair nymphs, this shadow soon, too soon, will
   reach

The front now bright of that descended Goddess.
Her lost one she hath found—alas, too late.
Seeds of a Stygian fruit have passed her lips!
Three fatal seeds! Proserpina hath sucked
Into her being, the dark element.
And yet lament not; Ceres' self shall learn
Comfort and divine solace from her child.
What the Gods could not give, her child, though sad,
Yet fraught with sweetness of Elysian wisdom,
Bestows upon the Mother. From this hour
Let every mortal Mother that hath given
A child from her own heart into the Shades,
Live and take comfort; they shall meet again.
Let every mourner in the Past who buries
An innocent delight, be sure henceforth
That in the Future a large treasure-house,
It doth await him. Gentle Nymphs, weep not;
Those parted lips, those smooth and candid brows
Were not for mourners fashioned, sigh or shadow,
But for pure breathing of celestial airs,
And gracing a light garland.

NYMPHS.

Mild-eyed Goddess!
Must we no more behold Proserpina?
Must flower-famed Sicily have no more flowers?

IRIS.

I see the end, and therefore I am glad,
I that look down into the smallest dewdrop,
Yet in my bright arch clasp the end of all:
And, whether I descend, the adorned cradle
Of some young flower to rock, or fatally
To cut the locks of some expiring King,
My task is kind, and Comforter my name.
Fear nought; Proserpina shall rise once more;
For Jove is clement; and a Mother's prayers
Ofttimes of fateful power against the Fates.
One half the year in darkness dwells she throned
A Queen; one half she plays, a child on Earth,
Flower-crowned, and constant 'mid inconstancy,
Whether Narcissus now, or Daffodil
Her choice persuade; or mysteries in the cups
Of Cowslips through thick honey scarce espied,
Or Primroses moon-lighted all day long,
Or fabled Pansy, or Anemone
Wind-chidden, or the red all-conquering Rose,
Enchain her youthful heart—or other flowers,
Named on the Earth but nameless still in Heaven,
Subdue her, each in turn or all at once.
Mild nymphs, farewell! To Juno, large-eyed Queen,
Whose Herald fair I boast myself, once more
I speed.

(*Nymphs descend, singing.*)

Strophe.

Proserpina once more
  Will come to us a-Maying;
Sicilian meadows o'er
  Low-singing and light-playing,
The wintry durance past,
Delight will come at last:
Proserpina will come to us—
  Will come to us a-Maying.

Antistrophe.

Sullen skies to-day,
  Sunny skies to-morrow;
November steals from May,
  And May from her doth borrow;
Griefs—Joys—in Time's strange dance
Interchangeably advance;
The sweetest joys that come to us
  Come sweeter for past sorrow.

GREEK IDYLLS.

I.—*GLAUCÈ*.

I LOVE you, pretty maid, for you are young:
I love you, pretty maid, for you are fair:
I love you, pretty maid, for you love me.

They tell me that, a babe, smiling you gazed
Upon the stars, with open, asking eyes,
And tremulous lips apart. Erelong, self-taught,
You found for every star and every flower
Legends and names and fables sweet and new.

O that when far away I still might see thee!
How oft when wearied with the din of life
On thee mine eyes would rest, thy Grecian heavens
Brightening that orbèd brow—
Hesper should shine upon thee, lamp of Love,
Beneath whose radiance thou wert born. O Hesper!
Thee will I love and reverence evermore.

Bind up that shining hair into a knot
And let me see that polished neck of thine
Uprising from the bed snow-soft, snow-white
In which it rests so gracefully! What God
Hath drawn upon thy forehead's ivory plane

Those two clear streaks of sweet and glistening
    black
Lifted in earnest mirth or lovely awe?
Open those Pleiad eyes, liquid and tender,
And let me lose myself among their depths!
Caress me with thy infant hands, and tell me
Old tales divine that love makes ever new
Of Gods and men entoiled in flowery nets,
Of heroes sighing all their youth away,
And Troy, death-sentenced by those Argive eyes.

Come forth, dear maid, the day is calm and cool,
And bright though sunless. Like a long green
    scarf,
The tall Pines crowning yon grey promontory
In distant ether hang, and cut the sea.
But lovers better love the dell, for there
Each is the other's world. How indolently
The tops of those pale poplars bend and sway
Over the violet-braided river's brim!
Whence comes their motion, for no wind is heard,
And the long grasses move not, nor the reeds?
Here we will sit, and watch the rushes lying
Like locks along the leaden-coloured stream
Far off—and thou, O child, shalt talk to me
Of Naiads and their loves. A blissful life
They lead, who live beneath the flowing waters:
They cherish calm and think the sea-weeds fair;

They love each other's beauty; love to stand
Among the lilies, holding back their tresses
And listening, with their gentle cheek reclined
Upon the flood to some far melody
Of Pan or shepherd piping in lone woods,
Until the unconscious tears run down their face.
Mild are their loves, nor burdensome their
    thoughts—
I would that such a life were mine and thine!

II.—*IONÈ*.

Ionè, fifteen years have o'er you passed,
And, taking nothing from you in their flight,
Have given you much. You look like one for whom
The day has morning only, time but Spring.
Your eyes are large and calm, your lips serene,
As if no Winter with your dreams commingled,
You that dream always, or that never dream!

Dear maid, you should have been a shepherdess—
But no: ill tended then your flocks had strayed.
Young fawns you should have led; such fawns as
    once
The quivered Queen had spared to startle! Then
Within your hand a willow wand,-your brow
Wreathed with red roses heavier for warm rains,

How sweetly, with half-serious countenance,
Through the green alleys had you ta'en your way!
And they, your spotted train, how happily
Would they have gambolled by you—happiest she
The milk-white creature in the silver chain!

Ionè, lay the tapestry down : come forth—
No golden ringlet shall you add this morn
To bright Apollo : and poor Daphne there!
Without her verdant branches she must rest
Another day—a cruel tale, sweet girl!

You will not ? Then farewell our loves for ever!
We are too far unlike : not Cyclops more
Unlike that Galatea whom he wooed.
I love the loud-resounding sea divine ;
I love the wintry sunset, and the stress
Inexorable of wide-wasting storms ;
I love the waste of foam-washed promontories,
The singing of the topmost mountain pines
In safety heard far down, the ringing sleet,
Thunder, and all portentous change that makes
The mind of mortals like to suns eclipsed
Waning in icy terrors. These to you
Are nothing. On the ivied banks you lie
In deep green valleys grey with noontide dew :
There bathe your feet in bubbling springs, your
    hands
Playing with the moist pansies near your face.

These bowers are musical with nightingales
Morning and noon and night. Among these rocks
A lovely life is that you lead; but I
Will make it lovelier with some pretty gift
If you are constant to me! Constant never
Was Nymph or Nereid: like the waves they change,
O Nymph, so change not thou! A boat I'll make
Scooped from a pine; yourself shall learn to row it
Swifter than winds or sounds can fleet; or else
Your scarf shall be the sail, and you shall glide,
While the stars drop their light upon the bay,
On like a bird between the double heaven.
Are these but trivial joys? Ah me! fresh leaves
Gladden the forests, but no second life
Invests our branches; feathers new make bright
The birds, but when our affluent locks desert us
No Spring restores them. Dried-up streams once more
The laughing Nymphs replenish, but man's life,
By fate drawn down and smothered in the sands,
Never looks up. Alas, my sweet Ionè,
Alcæus also loved; but in his arms
Finds rest no more the songful Lesbian maid,
Her breast all shaken by the storm of song,
Or thrills of song unborn!
The indignant hand attesting Gods and men
Achilles lifts no more; to dust is turned

His harp that glittered through the wild sea spray
Though the black wave falls yet on Ilion's shore.
All things must die—the Songs themselves, except
The devout hymn of grateful love ; or hers,
The wild swan's, chanting her death melody.

III.—*LYCIUS.*

Lycius! the female race is all the same !
All variable, as the Poets tell us ;
Mad through caprice—half way 'twixt men and
    children.

Acasta, mildest late of all our maids,
Colder and calmer than a sacred well,
Is now more changed than Spring has changed
    these woods ;
Hers is the fault, not mine. Yourself shall judge.

From Epidaurus, where for three long days
With Nicias I had stayed, honouring the God,
Last evening we returned. The way was dull
And vexed with mountains: tired ere long was I
From warding off the oleander boughs
Which, as my comrade o'er the stream's dry bed
Pushed on, closed backward on my mule and me ;
The flies maintained a melody unblest ;

While Nicias, of his wreath Nemean proud,
Sang of the Satyrs and the Nymphs all day
Like one by Æsculapius fever-smitten.
Arrived at eve, we bathed and drank, and ate
Of figs and olives till our souls exulted:
Lastly we slept like Gods. When morning shone
So filled was I with weariness and sleep
That as a log till noon I lay, then rose
And in the bath-room sat. While there I languished
Reading that old, divine and holy tale
Of sad Ismenè and Antigonè,
Two warm soft hands around me sudden flung
Closed both my eyes; and a clear, shrill, sweet laughter
Told me that she it was, Acasta's self,
That brake upon my dreams. 'What would you, child?'
'Child, Child,' Acasta cried! 'I am no child—
You do me wrong in calling me a child!
Come with me to the willowy river's brim:
There read, if you must read.'

                          Her eyes not less
Than hands uplifted me, and forth we strayed.
O'er all the Argolic plain Apollo's shafts
So fiercely fell, methought the least had slain
A second Python. From that theatre

Hewn in the rock the Argive tumult rolled :
Before the fane of Juno seven vast oxen
Lowed loud, denouncing Heaven ere yet they fell ;
While from the hill-girt meadows rose a scent
So rich, the salt sea odours vainly strove
To pierce those fumes it curled about my brain,
And sting the nimbler spirits. Nodding I watched
The pale herbs from the parchèd bank that trailed
Bathing delighted in voluptuous cold
And scarcely swayed by the slow winding stream.
I heard a sigh—I asked not whence it came.
At last a breeze went by, to glossy waves
Rippling the steely flood ; I noted then
The reflex of the poplar stem thereon
Curled into spiral wreaths and toward me darting
Like a long, shining water-snake : I laughed
To see its restlessness. Acasta cried
' Read—if you will not speak or look at me ! '
Unconsciously I glanced upon the page,
Bent o'er it, and began to chant that song
'Favoured by Love are they that love not deeply,'
When leaping from my side she snatched the scroll,
Into the river dashed it, bounded by,
And, no word spoken, left me there alone.

Lycius ! I see you smile ; but know you not
Nothing is trifling which the Muse records,
And lovers love to muse on ? Let the Gods

Act as to them seems fitting. Hermes loved—
Phœbus loved also—but the hearts of Gods
Are everlasting like the suns and stars.
Their loves as transient as the clouds. For me
A peaceful life is all I seek, and far
Removed from cares and from the female kind!

ODE TO THE DAFFODIL.

I.

O LOVE-STAR of the unbelovèd March,
   When, cold and shrill,
Forth flows beneath a low, dim-lighted arch
   The wind that beats sharp crag and barren hill
   And keeps unfilmed the lately torpid rill!

II.

   A week or e'er
Thou com'st thy soul is round us everywhere,
   And many an auspice, many an omen,
   Whispers, scarce noted, thou art coming:
Huge, cloudlike trees grow dense with sprays and buds
   And cast a shapelier gloom o'er freshening grass;
And through the fringe of ragged woods
   More shrouded sunbeams pass:

Fresh shoots conceal the pollard's spike
   The driving rack out-braving;
The hedge swells large by ditch and dike;
And all the uncoloured world is like
   A shadow-limned engraving.

III.

Herald and harbinger! with thee
Begins the year's great jubilee!
   Of her solemnities sublime
A sacristan whose gusty taper
Flashes through earliest morning vapour
   Thou ring'st dark nocturns and dim prime.
Birds that have yet no heart for song
   Gain strength with thee to twitter;
And, warm at last, where hollies throng
   The mirrored sunbeams glitter.
With silk the osier plumes her tendrils thin:
   Sweet blasts, though keen as sweet, the blue
      lake wrinkle:
And buds on leafless boughs begin
   Against grey skies to twinkle.

IV.

   To thee belongs
A pathos drowned in later scents and songs!
Thou com'st when first the Spring
   On Winter's verge encroaches;

When gifts that speed on wounded wing
   Meet little save reproaches!
Thou com'st when blossoms blighted
   Retracted sweets, and ditty
From suppliants oft deceived and spited
   More anger draw than pity!
Thee the old shepherd on the bleak hill-side
   Far distant eyeing leans upon his staff
Till from his cheek the wind-brushed tear is dried.
   In thee he spells his boyhood's epitaph.
To thee belongs the youngling of the flock
   When first it lies, close-huddled from the cold,
Between the sheltering rock
   And gorse-bush slowly overcrept with gold.

v.

Thou laugh'st, bold outcast bright as brave,
When the wood bellows and the cave,
And leagues inland is heard the wave!
   Hating the dainty and the fine
   As sings the blackbird thou dost shine!
Thou com'st while yet on mountain lawns high up
   Lurks the last snow, while by the berried breer
As yet the black spring in its craggy cup
   No music makes or charms no listening ear.
Thou com'st while from the oak stock or red beech
Dead Autumn scoffs young Spring with splenetic
       speech ;

When in her vidual chastity the Year
With frozen memories of the sacred past
Her doors and heart makes fast,
And loves no flower save those that deck the bier :
   Ere yet the blossomed sycamore
   With golden surf is curdled o'er ;
   Ere yet the birch against the blue
   Her silken tissue weaves anew.
Thou com'st while, meteor-like 'mid fens, the weed
   Swims wan in light ; while sleet-showers
      whitening glare ;
Weeks ere by river brims, new furred, the reed
   Leans its green javelin level in the air.

VI.

   Child of the strong and strenuous East !
Now scattered wide o'er dusk hill bases,
Now massed in broad illuminate spaces ;
   Torchbearer at a wedding feast
Whereof thou mayst not be partaker,
But mime, at most, and merrymaker ;
Phosphor of an ungrateful sun
That rises but to bid thy lamp begone :—
            Farewell ! I saw
Writ large on woods and lawns to-day that Law
Which back remands thy race and thee
To hero-haunted shades of dark Persephonè.
To-day the Spring has pledged her marriage vow :

Her voice, late tremulous, strong has grown and
    steady :
To-day the Spring is crowned a queen : but thou
    Thy winter hast already !
Take my song's blessing, and depart,
    Type of true service—unrequited heart.

SONG.

I.

Softly, O midnight Hours !
Move softly o'er the bowers
Where lies in happy sleep a girl so fair !
    For ye have power, men say,
    Our hearts in sleep to sway,
And cage cold fancies in a moonlight snare.
    Round ivory neck and arm
    Enclasp a separate charm :
Hang o'er her poised ; but breathe nor sigh nor
    prayer :
    Silently ye may smile,
    But hold your breath the while,
And let the wind sweep back your cloudy hair !

II.

Bend down your glittering urns
Ere yet the dawn returns

And star with dew the lawn her feet shall tread;
    Upon the air rain balm;
    Bid all the woods be calm;
Ambrosial dreams with healthful slumbers wed;
    That so the Maiden may
    With smiles your care repay
When from her couch she lifts her golden head;
    Waking with earliest birds,
    Ere yet the misty herds
Leave warm 'mid the grey grass their dusky bed.

LOVE AND SORROW.

Wherever under bowers of myrtle
    Love, summer-tressed and vernal-eyed,
At morn or eve is seen to wander
    A dark-eyed girl is at his side.

No eye beholds the Virgin gliding
    Unsandalled through the thicket's glooms;
Yet some have marked her shadow moving
    Like twilight o'er the whiter blooms.

A golden bow the Brother carries,
    A silver flute the Sister bears:
And ever at the fatal moment
    The notes and arrows fly in pairs.

She rests her flute upon her bosom
    While up to heaven his bow he rears,
And as her kisses make it tremble
    That flute is moistened by her tears.

The lovely twain were born together,
    And in the same shell-cradle laid,
By one sea-murmur lulled to slumber,
    Together slept, and sleeping played

With hands into each other's woven
    And whispering lips that seem to teach
Each other in their rosy motion
    What still their favourites learn from each.

Proud of her boy, the Mother showed him
    To mortal and immortal eye;
But hid, because she loved her dearer,
    The deeper, sweeter Mystery.

Accept them both, or hope for neither,
    Love-seeking Youth or Maid love-lorn,
For Grief has come where Love is welcome,
    And Love will comfort those who mourn.

DEATH IN CHILDBIRTH.

Sweet Martyr of thine Infant and thy Love,
  O what a death is thine !
Is this to die ?   Then, Love ! henceforth approve
  This, this of all thy gifts the most divine !
Grave she needs not : Matrons, cover
  Her white bed with flowers all over ;
With the dark, cool violets swathing
  A full bosom mother-hearted ;
Under lily shadows bathing
  Brows whose anguish hath departed.
Life with others, Death with thee
Plays a grave game smilingly—
O Death not Death ! through worlds of bliss
  The happy new-born Soul is straying !
O Death not Death ! thy Babe in this,
  An Angel on the earth, is playing !

THE DIGNITY OF SORROW.

I.

I have not seen you since the Shadow fell
  From Heaven against your door ;
I know not if you bear your sorrow well ;
  I only know your hearth is cold ; your floor
  Will feel that soft and gliding tread no more.

II.

I know our ancient friendship now is over;
   I can love still and so will not complain;
     I have not loved in vain;
Taught long that Art of Sadness to discover
   Which draws stern solace from the wells of pain.
You love the dead alone;—or you have lost
The power and life of Love in time's untimely
     frost.

III.

You have stood up in the great Monarch's court—
   The court of Death; in spirit you have seen
     His lonely shades serene
Where all the mighty men of old resort:
     The eyes of Proserpine
Heavy and black have rested upon thine.
Her vintage, wine from laurel-berries prest,
   You raised—and laid you then the chalice down
   Scared by that Queen's inevitable frown,
Just as the marble touched your panting breast?
   O! in the mirror of that poison cold
   What Shadow or what Shape did you behold?

IV.

And she is dead: and you have long been dying;
   And are recovered, and live on. O, Friend;
     Say, what shall be the end
Of leaf-lamenting boughs and wintry sighing?

When will the woods that moan
      Resume their green array ?
   When will the dull, sad clouds be over blown,
      And a calm sunset close our stormy day ?

V.

   My thoughts pursue you still : I call them back :
      Once more they seek you, like the birds that rise
   From reedy bank, and in a winding track
      Circle the field in which their forage lies ;
   Or like some poor and downcast Pensioner
      Depressed and timid though his head be grey,
         That moves with curving steps to greet his Lord
      Whom he hath watched all day—
   .   Yet lets him pass away without a word ;
   And gazes on his footsteps from afar.

LOVE AND COUNSEL.

   A NIGHTINGALE fell sick among the leaves :
      There came to it a little envious thrush
   And said, 'I know a cure for one who grieves ;
      'The chill, black berry on the laurel bush.'

The Nightingale, love-wearied, ate and died.
  Cold comforter! I scorn thy counsel's lure:
Near her I grieve, but live: To leave her side
  Were death: my wound is better than thy cure.

ODE TO IRELAND.
(AGAINST FALSE FREEDOM.)
1860.

I.

The Nations have their parts assigned:
The deaf one watches for the blind:
The blind for him that hears not hears:
Harmonious as the heavenly spheres
Despite external fret and jar
Their mutual ministrations are.
Some shine on history's earlier page;
Some prop the world's declining age:
One, one reserves her buried bloom
To flower—perchance on Winter's tomb.

II.

Greece, weak of Will but strong in Thought,
To Rome her arts and science brought;

Rome, strong yet barbarous, gained from her
A staff; but, like Saint Christopher,
Knew not for whom his strength to use,
What yoke to bear, what master choose.
His neck the giant bent!—thereon
The Babe of Bethlehem sat! Anon
That staff his prop, that sacred freight
His guide, he waded through the strait,
And entered at a new world's gate.

III.

On that new stage were played once more
The parts in Greece rehearsed before:
Round fame's Olympic stadium vast
Again the emulous Nations raced;
Now Spain, now France the headship won,
Unrisen the Russian Macedon:
But nought, O Ireland, like to thee
Hath been! A Sphinx-like mystery,
At the world's feast thou sat'st death-pale;
And blood-stains tinged thy widowed veil.

IV.

Apostle, first, of worlds unseen!
For ages, then, deject and mean;
Be sure, sad land, a concord lay
Between thy darkness and thy day.

Thy hand, had temporal gifts been thine,
Had lost, perchance, the things divine.
Truth's witness sole! The insurgent North
Gave way when Error's flood went forth :
On the scarred coasts deformed and cleft
Thou, like the Church's Rock, wert left.

V.

That Tudor tyranny which stood
'Mid wrecks of Faith, was quenched in blood
When Charles its child and victim lay
The Rebel-Prophet's bleeding prey.
Once more the unhappy wheel goes round!
Heads royal long are half discrowned :
Ancestral rights decline and die :—
Thus Despotism and Anarchy
Alternate each the other chase,
Twin Bacchantes wreathed around one vase.

VI.

The future sleeps in night : but thou
O Island of the branded brow,
Her flatteries scorn who reared by Seine
Fraternity's ensanguined reign
And for a sceptre twice abhorred
Twice welcomed the Cæsarian sword!

Thy past, thy hope, are thine alone !
Though crushed around thee and o'erthrown
The majesty of civil might
The hierarchy of social right
Firm state in thee for ever hold !
Religion was their life and mould.

V.I.

The vulgar, dog-like eye can see
Only the ignobler traits in thee ;
Quaint follies of a fleeting time ;
Dark reliques of the oppressor's crime.
The Seer—What sees he ? What the West
Hath seldom save in thee possessed ;
The childlike Faith ; the Will like fate,
And that Theistic Instinct great
New worlds that summons from the abyss
'The balance to redress of this.'

VIII.

Wait thou the end ; and spurn the while
False Freedom's meretricious smile !
Stoop not thy front to anticipate
Faith's triumph certain ! Watch and wait !
The schismatic, by blood akin
To Socialist and Jacobin,
Will claim, when shift the scales of power,
His natural place. Be thine that hour

With good his evil to requite ;
To save him in his own despite ;
And backward scare the brood of night !

THE BARD ETHELL.
IRELAND, 13TH CENTURY.

I.

I am Ethell, the son of Conn ;
  Here I live at the foot of the hill ;
I am clansman to Brian and servant to none ;
  Whom I hated I hate, whom I loved love still.
Blind am I. On milk I live,
  And meat, God sends it, on each Saint's day,
Though Donald Mac Art—may he never thrive—
  Last Shrovetide drove half my kine away !

II.

At the brown hill's base by the pale blue lake
  I dwell, and see the things I saw ;
The heron flap heavily up from the brake,
  The crow fly homeward with twig or straw,
The wild duck, a silver line in wake,
  Cutting the calm mere to far Bunaw.

And the things that I heard, though deaf I hear;
From the tower in the island the feastful cheer;
The horn from the wood; the plunge of the stag
With the loud hounds after him down from the
    crag.
Sweet is the chase, but the battle is sweeter;
More healthful, more joyous, for true men meeter!

III.

My hand is weak! it once was strong:
    My heart burns still with its ancient fire;
If any man smites me he does me wrong
For I was the Bard of Brian Mac Guire.
If any man slay me—not unaware,
    By no chance blow, nor in wine and revel—
I have stored beforehand a curse in my prayer
    For his kith and kindred: his deed is evil.

IV.

There never was King, and there never will be,
In battle or banquet like Malachi!
The Seers his reign had predicted long;
He honoured the Bards, and gave gold for song.
If rebels arose, he put out their eyes;
    If robbers plundered or burned the fanes
He hung them in chaplets like rosaries
    That others, beholding, might take more pains:

There was none to woman more reverent-minded
  For he held his mother, and Mary, dear;
If any man wronged them that man he blinded,
  Or straight amerced him of hand or ear.
There was none who founded more convents—
    none:
  In his palace the old and the poor were fed;
The orphan walked, and the widow's son,
  Without groom or page to his throne or bed.
In council he mused with great brows divine
And eyes like the eyes of the musing kine,
Upholding a Sceptre o'er which men said
Seven Spirits of Wisdom like fire-tongues played.
He drained ten lakes and he built ten bridges;
  He bought a gold book for a thousand cows;
He slew ten Princes who brake their pledges;
  With the bribed and the base he scorned to
    carouse.
He was sweet and awful; through all his reign
God gave great harvests to vale and plain;
From his nurse's milk he was kind and brave;
And when he went down to his well-wept grave
Through the triumph of penance his soul uprose
To God and the Saints. Not so his foes!

v.

The King that came after! ah woe, woe, woe!
He doubted his friend and he trusted his foe;

He bought and he sold ; his kingdom old
  He pledged and pawned to avenge a spite ;
No bard or prophet his birth foretold ;
  He was guarded and warded both day and night ;
He counselled with fools and had boors at his feast ;
He was cruel to Christian and kind to beast ;
Men smiled when they talked of him far o'er the
    wave ;
Well paid were the mourners that wept at his
    grave.
God plagued for his sake his people sore :
  They sinned ; for the people should watch and
    pray
That their prayers like angels at window and door
  May keep from the King the bad thought away !

VI.

The sun has risen : on lip and brow
  He greets me—I feel it—with golden wand ;
Ah, bright-faced Norna ! I see thee now ;
  Where first I saw thee I see thee stand.
From the trellis the girl looked down on me ;
  Her maidens stood near ; it was late in spring ;
The grey priests laughed as she cried in glee
  ' Good Bard, a song in my honour sing ! '
I sang her praise in a loud-voiced hymn
To God who had fashioned her, face and limb,

For the praise of the clan and the land's behoof :
So she flung me a flower from the trellis roof.
Ere long I saw her the hill descending ;
   O'er the lake the May morning rose moist and
      slow ;
She prayed me, her smile with the sweet voice
      blending,
   To teach her all that a woman should know.
Panting she stood ; she was out of breath ;
   The wave of her little breast was shaking ;
From eyes still childish and dark as death
   Came womanhood's dawn thro' a dew-cloud
      breaking.
Norna was never long time the same :
   By a spirit so strong was her slight form moulded
The curves swelled out from the flower-like frame
   In joy; in grief to a bud she folded :
When she listened her eyes grew bright and large
Like springs rain-fed that dilate their marge.

VII.

So I taught her the hymn of Patrick the Apostle
   And the marvels of Bridget and Columkille ;
Ere long she sang like the lark or the throstle,
   Sang the deeds of the servants of God's high
      Will :
I told her of Brendan who found afar
Another world 'neath the western star ;

Of our three great bishops in Lindisfarne isle;
Of St. Fursey the wondrous, Fiacre without guile;
Of Sedulius, hymn-maker when hymns were rare;
Of Scotus the subtle, who clove a hair
Into sixty parts, and had marge to spare:
To her brother I spake of Oisin and Fionn,
And they wept at the death of great Oisin's son;[*]
I taught the heart of the boy to revel
  In tales of old greatness that never tire;
And the virgin's, upspringing from earth's low level,
  To wed with heaven like the altar fire.
I taught her all that a woman should know;
  And that none might teach her worse lore, I gave her
A dagger keen, and taught her the blow
  That subdues the knave to discreet behaviour:
A sand-stone there on my knee she set,
And sharpened its point—I can see her yet—
I held back her hair, and she sharpened the edge
While the wind piped low through the reeds and
  sedge.

VIII.

She died in the convent on Ina's height:—
  I saw her the day when she took the veil;
As slender she stood as the Paschal light,
  As tall and slender and bright and pale.

[*] Ossian's son, Oscar.

I saw her; and dropped as dead : bereaven
Is earth when her holy ones leave her for heaven :
Her brother fell in the fight at Beigh :
May they plead for me, both, on my dying day!

IX.

All praise to the man who brought us the
    Faith!
'Tis a staff by day and our pillow in death.
All praise, I say, to that blessed youth
    Who heard in a dream from Tyrawley's strand
    That wail, 'Put forth o'er the sea thy hand;
In the dark we die; give us Hope and Truth!'
But Patrick built not on Iorras' shore
    That convent where now the Franciscans
    dwell :
Columba was mighty in prayer and war;
    But the young monk preaches, as loud as his
    bell
That love must rule all, and wrongs be forgiven
Or else, he is sure, we shall reach not, Heaven!
That doctrine, I count right cruel and hard:
And when I am laid in the old churchyard
The habit of Francis I will not wear;
Nor wear I his cord, or his cloth of hair
In secret. Men dwindle : till psalm and prayer
Had softened the land, no Dane dwelt there!

X.

I forgive old Cathbar who sank my boat :
Must I pardon Feargal who slew my son ;
Or the pirate Strongbow, who burned Granote,
   They tell me, and in it nine priests, a nun,
And—worst—Saint Finian's crosier staff ?
At forgiveness like that I spit and laugh !
My chief, in his wine-cups, forgave twelve men ;
And of these a dozen rebelled again !
There never was chief more brave than he !
   The night he was born Loch Gur up-burst ;
He was bard-loving, gift-making, loud of glee,
   The last to fly, to advance the first ;
He was like the top spray upon Uladh's oak,
   He was like the tap-root of Argial's pine ;
He was secret and sudden ; as lightning his stroke ;
   There was none that could fathom his hid design !
He slept not : if any man scorned his alliance
He struck the first blow for a frank defiance
With that look in his face, half night, half light,
Like the lake gust-blackened yet ridged with white !
There were comely wonders before he died ;
The eagle barked and the Banshee cried ;
The witch-elm wept with a blighted bud ;
The spray of the torrent was red with blood :
The chief, returned from the mountain's bound,
Forgat to ask after Bran, his hound.

We knew he would die ; three days passed o'er ;—
He died. We *waked* him for three days more.
One by one, upon brow and breast
The whole clan kissed him. In peace may he rest !

XI.

I sang his dirge. I could sing that time
Four thousand staves of ancestral rhyme :
To-day I can scarcely sing the half :
Of old I was corn, and now I am chaff.
My song to-day is a breeze that shakes
   Feebly the down on the cygnet's breast;
'Twas then a billow the beach that rakes
   Or a storm that buffets the mountain's crest.
Whatever I bit with a venomed song
   Grew sick, were it beast, or tree, or man :
The wronged one sued me to right his wrong
   With the flail of the Satire and fierce Ode's fan.
I sang to the chieftains : each stock I traced
Lest lines should grow tangled through fraud or
      haste.
To princes I sang in a loftier tone
Of Moran the Just who refused a throne ;
Of Moran whose torque would close and choke
The wry-necked witness that falsely spoke.
I taught them how to win love and hate
Not love from all ; and to shun debate.

To maids in the bower I sang of love ;
And of war at the feastings in bawn or grove.

XII.

How long He leaves me—the great God—here !
  Have I sinned some sin, or has God forgotten ?
This year I think is my hundredth year :
  I am like a bad apple, unripe yet rotten !
They shall lift me ere long, they shall lay me— the clan—
By the strength of men on Mount Cruachan !
God has much to think of ! How much He has seen
And how much is gone by that once has been !
On sandy hills where the rabbits burrow
  Are Raths of Kings men name not now ;
On mountain tops I have tracked the furrow
  And found in forests the buried plough.
For one now living the strong land then
Gave kindly food and raiment to ten.
No doubt they waxed proud and their God defied ;
  So their harvest He blighted or burned their hoard ;
Or He sent them plague, or He sent the sword ;
Or He sent them lightning ; and so they died
Like Dathi, the king, on the dark Alp's side.

XIII.

Ah me! that man who is made of dust
   Should have pride toward God! 'Tis a demon's
     spleen!
I have often feared lest God, the All-just,
   Should bend from heaven and sweep earth
     clean,
Should sweep us all into corners and holes,
Like dust of the house-floor, both bodies and
     souls.
I have often feared He would send some wind
In wrath, and the nation wake up stone-blind.
In age or in youth we have all wrought ill:
I say not our great king Nial did well
Although he was Lord of the Pledges Nine,
   When, beside subduing this land of Eire,
He raised in Armorica banner and sign
   And wasted the British coast with fire.
Perhaps in His mercy the Lord will say,
'These men! God's help! 'Twas a rough boy
     play!'
He is certain that young Franciscan Priest,
God sees great sin where men see least:
Yet this were to give unto God the eye,
Unmeet the thought—of the humming fly!
I trust there are small things He scorns to see
In the lowly who cry to Him piteously.
Our hope is Christ. I have wept full oft

He came not to Eire in Oisin's time;
Though love and those new monks would make
    men soft
If they were not hardened by war and rhyme.
I have done my part : my end draws nigh :
I shall leave old Eire with a smile and sigh :
She will miss not me as I missed my son :
Yet for her, and her praise, were my best deeds
    done.
Man's deeds! man's deeds! they are shades that
    fleet,
Or ripples like those that break at my feet :
The deeds of my Chief and the deeds of my
    King
Grow hazy, far seen, like the hills in spring.
Nothing is great save the death on the Cross !
    But Pilate and Herod I hate and know
    Had Fionn lived then he had laid them low
Though the world thereby had sustained great
    loss.
My blindness and deafness and aching back
With meekness I bear for that suffering's sake ;
And the Lent-fast for Mary's sake I love,
And the honour of Him the Man above !
My songs are all over now :—so best !
They are laid in the heavenly Singer's breast
Who never sings but a star is born :
May we hear his song in the endless morn !

I give glory to God for our battles won
   By wood or river, on bay or creek :
For Norna—who died ; for my father, Conn :
   For feasts, and the chase on the mountains bleak :
I bewail my sins, both unknown and known,
   And of those I have injured forgiveness seek.
The men that were wicked to me and mine—
Not quenching a wrong, nor in war or wine—
I forgive and absolve them all, save three:
May Christ in His mercy be kind to me !

THE WEDDING OF THE CLANS.

A GIRL'S BABBLE.

I go to knit two clans together ;
   Our clan and this clan unseen of yore :
Our clan fears nought ! but I go, O whither ?
   This day I go from my Mother's door.

Thou redbreast sing'st the old song over,
   Though many a time thou hast sung it before ;
They never sent thee to some strange new lover :
   I sing a new song by my Mother's door.

I stepped from my little room down by the ladder,
   The ladder that never so shook before ;
I was sad last night : to-day I am sadder
   Because I go from my Mother's door.

THE WEDDING OF THE CLANS.

The last snow melts upon bush and bramble;
   The gold bars shine on the forest's floor;
Shake not, thou leaf! it is I must tremble,
   Because I go from my Mother's door.

O weep no longer, my nurse and Mother!
   My foster-sister, weep not so sore!
You cannot come with me, Ir, my brother—
   Alone I go from my Mother's door.

Farewell, my wolf-hound, that slew Mac Owing
   As he caught me and far through the thickets
      bore:
My heifer, Alb, in the green vale lowing,
   My cygnet's nest upon Lorna's shore?

He has killed ten chiefs, this chief that plights me;
   His hand is like that of the giant Balor:
But I fear his kiss; and his beard affrights me,
   And the great stone dragon above his door.

Had I daughters nine with me they should tarry;
   They should sing old songs; they should dance
      at my door;
They should grind at the quern; no need to marry.
   O when will this marriage day be o'er?

UNA.

A "LOVELY fear," a sweet solicitude
For others' grief is hers; skilled are her fingers
To cool with dewy flowers the front of care
Flattering to pleasant tears the over-worn.
She lives in her sweet maidenhood, untouched
By doubt, distrust, or pain; and gives to Heaven
Her heart, to earth her pity, to her friends
The snow-fed fountains of her fresh affections;
Seldom she weeps, and never causes tears;
Her looks are gentle, and her voice as low
As morning winds that spare the trembling dewdrops;
Her hand is lighter than a young bird's wing.
You deem her undefended. She is strong!
A glorious Spirit zoned with power and beauty!
The pure are always strong; for they possess
Youth's Heaven-taught lore, and Virtue's might eterne:
And, as the ocean in the flowers of ocean,
So God within them dwells and moves around.

FROM PSYCHE; OR, AN OLD POET'S LOVE (1847).

I.

How blue were Ariadne's eyes
  When from the sea's horizon line
At eve she raised them on the skies!
  My Psyche, bluer far are thine.

How pallid, snatched from falling flowers,
  The cheek averse of Proserpine
Unshadowed yet by Stygian bowers!
  My Psyche, paler far is thine.

Yet thee no lover e'er forsook,
  No tyrant urged with love unkind:
Thy joy the ungentle cannot brook,
  Thy light would strike the unworthy blind.

A golden flame invests thy tresses:
  An azure flame invests thine eyes:
And well that wingless form expresses
  Communion with relinquished skies.

Forbear, O breezes of the West,
  To waft her to her native bourne;
For heavenly, by her feet impressed,
  Becomes our ancient earth outworn.

On Psyche's life our beings hang :
In Psyche life and love are one :—
My Psyche glanced at me and sang,
'Perhaps to-morrow I am gone !'

II.

PSYCHE'S STUDY.

The low sun smote the topmost rocks
   Ascending o'er the eastern sea :
Backward my Psyche waved her locks
   And held her book upon her knee.

No brake was near, no flower, no bird,
   No music but the ocean wave,
That with complacent murmur stirred
   The echoes of a neighbouring cave.

Absorbed my Pysche sat, her face
   Reflecting Plato's sun-like soul,
And seemed in every word to trace
   The pent-up spirit of the whole.

Absorbed she sat in breathless mood,
   Unmoved as kneeler at a shrine
Save one slight finger that pursued
   The meaning on from line to line.

As some white flower in forest nook
  Bends o'er its own face in a well ;
So seemed the virgin in that book
  Her soul, unread before, to spell.

Sudden, a crimson butterfly
  On that illumined page alit :—
My Pysche flung the volume by
  And sister-like, gave chase to it.

III.

Nearer yet, by soft degrees,
  Nearer nestling by my side,
Her arm she propped upon my knees,
  Her head, ere long, its place supplied.

Mysteriously a child there lurked
  Within that soaring spirit wild :
Mysteriously a woman worked
  Imprisoned in that fearless child.

One thought before me, like a star,
  Rolled onward ever, always on ;
It called me to the fields afar,
  In which triumphant palms are won.

The concourse of far years I heard
  Applausive as a summer sea :—
My trance was broken—Psyche stirred ;--
  ' Is Psyche nothing then to thee ? '

IV.

Ah, that a lightly-lifted hand
  Should thus man's soul depress or raise,
And wield as with a magic wand
  A spirit steeled in earlier days!

Ah, that a voice whose speech is song,
  Whose pathos weeps, whose gladness smiles,
Should melt a heart unmoved so long
  And charm it to the Syren Isles!

Ah, that one presence, morn or eve,
  Should fill deserted halls with light;
One breeze-like step departing leave
  The noonday darker than the night!

Thy power is great : but Love and Youth
  Conspire with thee; with thee they dwell;
From those kind eyes in tenderest ruth
  On mine they look and say 'Farewell!'

V.

PSYCHE SINGING.

Between the green hill and the cloud
  The skylark loosed his silver chain
Of rapturous music clear and loud;
  My Psyche answered back the strain!

A glory rushed along the sky ;
  She sang, and all dark things grew plain ;
Hope, star-like shone ; and Memory
  Flashed like a cypress gemmed with rain.

Once more the skylark recommenced ;
  Once more from heaven his challenge rang ;
Again with him my Psyche fenced ;
  At last the twain commingled sang.

Then first I learned the skylark's lore ;
  Then first the words he sang I knew,
My soul with rapture flooded o'er,
  As breeze-borne gossamer with dew.

VI.

My Psyche laid her silken hand
  Upon my silver head ;
And said, 'To thee shall I remand
  The light of seasons fled ?'

The child bent o'er me as she spake,
  And, leaning yet more near,
A tress that kissed me for Love's sake
  Removed from me a tear.

Psyche, not so ; lest life should grow
  Near thee too deeply sweet ;
And I, who censure Death as slow,
  Should fear her far-off feet.

Eternal sweetness, love, and truth,
　Are in thy face enshrined;
The breathing soul of endless youth
　On wafts thee like a wind.

Those eyes, where'er they chance to gaze,
　Might wake to songs the dumb;
Breathe thou upon my blighted bays—
　Rose-odoured they become!

Yet go, and cheer a happier throng;
　For Death, a spouse dark-eyed,
On me her eyes hath levelled long,
　And calls me to her side.

O'er yon not distant coast even now
　What shape ascends? A Tomb.
Farewell, my Psyche! Why shouldst thou
　Be shadowed by its gloom?

VII.

Pure lip coralline, slightly stirred;
　Thus stir; but speak not! Love can see
On you the syllables unheard
　Which are his only melody.

Pure drooping lids; dark lashes wet
　With that unhoped-for, trembling tear;
Thus droop, thus meet; nor give me yet
　The eyes that I desire, yet fear.

Hands lightly clasped on meekest knee ;
   All-beauteous head, as by a spell
Bent forward ; loveliest form to me
   A lovely Soul made visible :—

Speak not ! move not ! More tender grows
   The heart, long musing. Night may plead
Perhaps, my part ; and, at its close,
   The morning bring me light indeed.

VIII.

'Such beauty was not born to die !'
   That thought above my fancy kept
Hovering like moonbeams tremulously ;
   And as its lustre waned, I slept.

Deep Love kept vigil. Where she sate
   Methought I sought her. Ah, the change !
Youth freezes at the frown of Fate ;
   And Time defied will have revenge.

The summer sunshine of her head
   Had changed to moonlight tresses grey :
O'er all her countenance was spread
   The twilight of a winter's day.

Dim as a misty tree ere morn,
   Sad as a tide-deserted strand,
She sate, with roseless lip forlorn ;—
   I knelt, and, reverent, kissed her hand.

I loved her. Whom I loved of yore
  A shape all lustrous from the skies,
I loved that hour; and loved far more,
  So sweet in this unjust disguise.

A human tenderness, a love
  More deep than loves of prosperous years,
Through all my spirit rose and strove,
  And, cloud-like, o'er her sank in tears.

IX.

She leaves us! Many a gentler breast
  Will mourn our common loss like me;
The babe her hand, her voice caressed,
  The lamb that couched beside her knee:

That touch thou lovest—the robe's far gleam—
  Thou shalt not find, thou dark-eyed fawn!
Thy light is lost, exultant stream;
  Dim woods, your sweetness is withdrawn.

Descend, dark heavens, and flood with rain
  Their crimson roofs; their silence rout;
Their vapour-laden branches strain,
  And force the smothered sadness out!

That so the ascended moon, when breaks
  The cloud, may light once more a scene
Fair as some cheek that suffering makes
  Only more tearfully serene:

That so the vale she loved may look
  Calm as some cloister roofed with snows
Wherein, unseen in shadowy nook,
  A buried Vestal finds repose.

A SONG OF AGE.

I.

Who mourns? Flow on, delicious breeze!
  Who mourns though youth and strength go by?
Fresh leaves invest the vernal trees,
  Fresh airs will drown my latest sigh :
This frame is but a part outworn
  Of earth's great Whole that lifts more high
A tempest-freshened brow each morn
  To meet pure beams and azure sky.

II.

Thou world-renewing breath, sweep on,
  And waft earth's sweetness o'er the wave !
That earth will circle round the sun
  When God takes back the life He gave!
To each his turn! Even now I feel
  The feet of children press my grave,
And one deep whisper o'er it steal—
  'The Soul is His who died to save.'.

AGE.

OLD age ! The sound is harsh, and grates :
  Yet Life's a semblance, not a Truth :
Time binds an hourly changing mask
On Souls in changeless light that bask—
Younger we grow when near the gates
  Of everlasting Youth !

TO BURNS'S 'HIGHLAND MARY.'

I.

O LOVED by him whom Scotland loves,
  Long loved, and honoured duly
By all who love the bard who sang
  So sweetly and so truly !
In cultured dales his song prevails ;
  Thrills o'er the eagle's aëry—
Has any caught that strain, nor sighed
  For Burns's 'Highland Mary'?

II.

His golden hours of youth were thine ;
  Those hours whose flight is fleetest :

Of all his songs to thee he gave
   The freshest and the sweetest.
Ere ripe the fruit, one branch he brake
   All rich with bloom and blossom ;
And shook its dews, its incense shook,
   Above thy brow and bosom !

III.

And when his Spring, alas, how soon !
   Had been by care subverted,
His Summer, like a god repulsed,
   Had from his gates departed ;
Beneath that evening star once more
   Star of his morn and even !
To thee his suppliant hands he spread,
   And hailed his love 'in heaven.'

IV.

And if his being in 'a waste
   Of shame' too oft was squandered,
And if too oft his feet ill-starred
   In ways erroneous wandered,
Ah ! still his spirit's spirit bathed
   In purity eternal ;
And all fair things through thee retained
   For him their aspect vernal !

V.

Nor less that tenderness remained
    Thy favouring love implanted;
Compunctious pity, yearnings vague
    For love to earth not granted;
Reserve with freedom, female grace
    Well matched with manly vigour
In songs where fancy twined her wreaths
    Round judgment's stalwart rigour.

VI.

A mute but strong appeal was made
    To him by feeblest creatures:
In his large heart had each a part
    That part had found in Nature's:
The wildered sheep, sagacious dog,
    Old horse reduced and crazy,
The field-mouse by the plough upturned,
    And violated daisy.

VII.

In him there burned that passionate glow
    All Nature's soul and savour,
Which gives its hue to every flower,
    To every fruit its flavour:
Nor less the kindred power he felt
    That love of all things human
Whereof the fiery centre is
    The love man bears to woman.

VIII.

He sang the dignity of man,
    Sang woman's grace and goodness,
Passed by the world's half-truths, her lies
    Pierced through with lance-like shrewdness.
Upon life's broad highways he stood,
    And aped nor Greek nor Roman ;
But snatched from heaven Promethean fire
    To glorify things common.

IX.

He sang of youth, he sang of age,
    Their joys, their griefs, their labours ;
Felt with, not for, the people; hailed
    All Scotland's sons his neighbours ;
And therefore all repeat his verse,
    Hot youth, or greybeard steady
The boatman on Loch Etive's wave,
    The shepherd on Ben Ledi.

X.

He sang from love of song ; his name
    Dunedin's cliff resounded :
He left her, faithful to a fame
    On truth and nature founded.
He sought true fame, not loud acclaim ;
    Himself and Time he trusted :
For laurels crackling in the flame
    His fine ear never lusted !

XI.

He loved, and reason had to love,
  The illustrious land that bore him :
Where'er he went, like heaven's broad tent
  A star-bright Past hung o'er him.
Each isle had fenced a saint recluse,
  Each tower a hero dying;
Down every mountain-gorge had rolled
  The flood of foemen flying.

XII.

From age to age that land had paid
  No alien throne submission ;
For feudal faith had been her Law,
  And Freedom her Tradition.
Where frowned the rocks had Freedom smiled,
  Sung, 'mid the shrill wind's whistle ;
So England prized her garden Rose,
  But Scotland loved her Thistle.

XIII.

Fair field alone the brave demand,
  And Scotland ne'er had lost it :
And honest prove the hate and love
  To objects meet adjusted.
Her will and way had ne'er been crossed
  In fatal contradiction ;
Nor loyalty to treason soured,
  Nor faith abused with fiction.

XIV.

Honour to Scotland and to Burns!
  In him she stands collected:
A thousand streams one river make—
  Thus Genius, heaven-directed,
Conjoins all separate veins of power
  In one great soul-creation;
Thus blends a million men to make
  The Poet of the nation!

XV.

Be green for aye, green bank and brae
  Around Montgomery's Castle!
Blow there, ye earliest flowers! and there
  Ye sweetest song-birds, nestle!
For there was ta'en that last farewell
  In hope indulged how blindly;
And there was given that long, last gaze
  'That dwelt' on him 'sae kindly.'

XVI.

No word of thine recorded stands;
  Few words that hour were spoken:
Two Bibles there were interchanged
  And some slight love-gift broken:
And there thy cold, faint hands he pressed
  Thy head, by dew-drops misted:
And kisses, ill-resisted first,
  At last were unresisted.

XVII.

Ah! cease—she died. He, too, is dead:
   Of all her girlish graces
Perhaps one severed tress remains:
   The rest stern Time effaces—
Dust lost in dust. Not so: a bloom
   Is hers that ne'er can wither;
And in that lay that lives for aye
   The twain live on together!

ODE ON THE ASCENT OF THE ALPS.

I.

All night as in my dreams I lay
   The shout of torrents without number
Was in my ears—'Away, away,
   No time have we for slumber!
The star-beams in our eddies play;
The moon is set: away, away!'
And round the hills in tumult borne
   Through echoing caves and gorges rocking
The voices of the night and morn
Are crying louder in their scorn,
   My tedious languor mocking.
Alas! in vain man's mortal limbs would rise
To join in elemental ecstasies

II.

'But thou, O Muse, our heavenly mate,
Unclogged art thou by fleshly weight!
Ascend; upbearing my desire
Among the mountains high and higher.
Leap from the glen upon the forest;
　Leap from the forest on the snow:
And while from snow to cloud thou soarest
　Send back thy song below!'

III.

I spake—Behold her o'er the broad lake flying
　Like a great Angel missioned to bestow
Some boon on men beneath in sadness lying:
　The waves are murmuring silver murmurs low:
　　Beneath the curdling wind
Green through the shades the waters rush and roll,
Or whitened only by the unfrequent shoal;
Lo! two dark hills, with darker yet behind,
Confront them, purple mountains almost black,
　Each behind each self-folded and withdrawn
Beneath the umbrage of yon cloudy rack—
　　That orange gleam! 'tis dawn!
Onward! the swan's flight with yon eagle's blending,
On, wingèd Muse, still forward and ascending!

H

IV.

That mighty sweep, one orbit of her flight,
Has over-curved the mountain's barrier height:
She sinks, she speeds on prosperous wing prevailing,
Broad lights below and changeful shadows sailing,
Over a vale upon whose breadth may shine
   Not noontide suns alone but suns of even,
Warming the rich fields in their red decline,
   The grey streams flushing with the hues of heaven.
In vain those Shepherds call; they cannot wake
   The echoes on this wide and cultured plain
Where spreads the river now into a lake
   Now curves through walnut meads its golden chain,
      In-isling here and there some spot
      With orchard, hive, and one fair cot,
      Or children dragging from their boat
      Into the flood some reverend goat—
O happy valley! cradle soft and deep
      For blissful life, calm sleep
And leisure, and affections free and wide,
Give me yon plough, that I with thee may bide,
      Or climb those stages hut-bestrown
      Vast steps of Summer's mountain-throne

Terrace o'er terrace rising, line o'er line,
Swathed in the light wreaths of the elaborate
  vine.
  On yonder loftiest steep, the last
    From whose green base the grey rocks rise,
  In random circle idly cast
    A happy household lies :
  Not far there sits the plighted maid ;
  Her locks a lover's fingers braid—
  Fair, fearless maiden ! cause for fear
  Is none, though he alone were near :
Indulge at will thy sweet security !
  He doth but that bold front incline
  And all those wind-tossed curls on thine
To catch from thy fresh lips their mountain
  purity !

V.

Up to lonelier, narrower valleys
  Winds an intricate ravine
Whence the latest snow-blast sallies
  Through black firs scarce seen.
I hear through clouds the Hunter's hollo—
I hear, but scarcely dare to follow
'Mid chaotic rocks and woods,
Such as in her lyric moods

Nature, like a Bacchante, flings
From half-shaped imaginings;
There lie two prostrate trunks entangled
Like intertwisted dragons strangled;
Yon glacier shines a prophet's robe;
While broken sceptre, throne, and globe
Are strewn as left by rival States
Of elemental Potentates:
Pale floats the mist, a wizard's shroud:
There looms the broad crag from the cloud,
A thunder-graven Sphinx's head, half blind
    Gazing on far lands through the freezing wind!

VI.

My song grows smoother, hearing
    A smooth-voiced female hymn
In verse alternate cheering
    The pass above me dim.
Behold them now, a band
Of maids descending hand in hand;
Singing softly, singing proudly
Low-toned anthems echoed loudly,
Martyr sufferings, mountain pleasures,
    Grave, religious, sweet affections,
Tuned with notes of ancient measures,
    Linked with patriot recollections!

The land is strong when such as these
  Inspire their lovers and their brothers :
The land is strong with such as these
  Her heroes' destined mothers !
Freedom from every hut
    Sends down a separate root :
And when base swords her branches cut
    With tenfold might they shoot.
Her Temples are of pine-woods made,
  Not Tyrian gold or Parian stone
With roofs of cedar gem-inlaid :
  There sits she, thence alone
To those dispensing her large love
Who share her solemn feast above,
Nor fear her icy halls, or zone
Of clouds with which she girds her own !

VII.

Mount higher, mount higher !
With rock-girdled gyre
  Behind each grey ridge
  And pine-feathered ledge
A vale is suspended ; mount higher, mount higher !

From rock to rock leaping
  The wild goats, they bound ;
The resinous odours
  Are wafted around ;

The clouds, disentangled,
With blue gaps are spangled ;
Green isles of the valley with sunshine are crowned.

The birches new budded
  Make pink the green copse ;
From the briar and hazel
  The crystal rain drops ;
    As he climbs, the boughs shaking,
    Nest-seeking, branch-breaking,
Beneath the white ash-boughs the shepherd-boy stops.

How happy that shepherd !
  How happy the lass !
How freshly beside them
  The pure Zephyrs pass !
    Sing, sing ! From the soil
    Springs bubble and boil,
And sun-smitten torrents fall soft on the grass.

Once more on every turf-clad stage
Peeps forth some household hermitage ;
Once more from tracts serene and high
The young lambs bleat, the dams reply.
From echoing trunks I hear the dash
Of headlong stream or 'Ranz des Vaches.'
Lo ! from thickets lightly springing
  An old church spire ; around its base

Devotions ever upward winging
  That find in Heaven their resting-place;
Around it grey-haired votaries kneel
  Who look along it to the skies,
And babes with imitative zeal
  Kissing their lip-worn rosaries.
Not soon the mountain Faith grows cold;
  Yon hamlet is six centuries old !

VIII.

Mount higher, mount higher,
  To the cloudland nigher !
    To the regions we climb
    Of our long-buried prime ;
In the skies it awaits us—Up higher, up higher !

  Loud Hymn and clear Pæan
    From the caverns are rolled :
  Far below us is Summer ;
    We have slipped from her fold ;
    We have passed, like a breath,
    To new life without death—
The Spring and our Childhood all round we behold.

IX.

What are toils to men who scorn them ?
  Perils what to men who dare ?

Chains to hands that once have torn them
　　Thenceforth are chains of air.
The winds above the snow-plains fleet;
Like them I race with wingèd feet:
My bonds are dropped; my spirit thrills,
A Freeman of the Eternal Hills!
Each cloud by turns I make my tent;
I run before the radiance sent
From every mountain's silver mail
Across dark gulfs from vale to vale:
The curdling mist in smooth career
　　A lovely phantom fleeting by
As silent sails through yon pale mere
　　That shrines its own blue sky;
The sun that mere makes now its targe,
And rainbow vapours tread its marge;
　　A whisper, such as lovers use,
Far off on those still heights was heard;
But here was never sound of bird;
　　No wild bee lets its murmur loose
O'er those blue flowers in rocky cleft
Their unvoluptuous eyes that lift
From feathery tufts of spangled moss
Pure as the snows which they emboss.
Lo! like the foam of wintry ocean,
　　The clouds beneath my feet are curled;
Dividing now with solemn motion
　　They give me back the world.

ODE ON THE ASCENT OF THE ALPS.

No veil I fear, no visual bond
In this aërial diamond:
My head o'er crystal bastions bent
'Twixt star-crowned spire and battlement,
I see the river of green ice
From precipice to precipice
Wind earthward slow, with blighting breath
Blackening the vales below like death.
Far, far beneath in sealike reach
   Receding to the horizon's rim
I see the woods of pine and beech,
   By their own breath made dim:
I see the land which heroes trod;
   I see the land where Virtue chose
To live alone, and live to God;
   The land she gave to those
Who know that on the hearth alone
True Freedom rears her fort and throne.

X.

Lift up not only hand and eye,
Lift up, O Man, thy heart on high:
Or downward gaze once more; and see
How spiritual dust can be!
Then far into the Future dive,
And ask if there indeed survive,
When fade the worlds, no primal shapes
Of disembodied hills and caves,

Types meet to shadow Godhead forth ;
Dread antitypes of shapes on earth ?
O Earth ! thou shalt not wholly die,
   Of some 'new Earth' the chrysalis
Predestined from Eternity,
   Nor seldom seen through this ;
On which, in glory gazing, we
Perchance shall oft remember thee,
And trace through it thine ancient frame
Distinct, like flame espied through flame,
Or like our earliest friends, above
Not lost though merged in heavenlier love—
How changed, yet still the same !

XI.

Here rest, my Soul, from meteor dreams ;
And thou, my Song, find rest. The streams
That left at morn yon mountain's brow
Are sleeping with Locarno now.
Earth seeks perforce from joy release,
   But Heaven in rapture finds her peace.
Gaze on those skies at once o'er all the earth
   Dissolving in a bath of purple dews,
And spread thy soul abroad as widely forth
     Till Love thy soul, as Heaven the snows,
   suffuse.

The sun is set—but upwards without end
  Two mighty beams, diverging,
Like hands in benediction raised, extend;
From the great deep a crimson mist is surging;
  The peaks are pyres where Day doth lie
  Like Indian widows, proud to die;
  Strange gleams, each moment ten times bright,
  Shoot round, transfiguring as they smite
  All spaces of the empyreal height;
Deep gleams, high Words which God to man doth
    speak;
  From peak to solemn peak in order driven
They speed—a loftier vision dost thou seek?
  Rise then to Heaven!

LINES WRITTEN UNDER DELPHI.

I.

My goal is reached—homeward henceforth my way.
I have beheld Earth's glories. Had the eyes
Of those I love reposed on them with mine
No future wish to roam beyond the range
Of one green pasture circling one clear lake
Itself by one soft woodland girt around,
Could touch this heart. My pilgrimage is made.

II.

I have seen Delphi ; I no more shall see it ;
I go contented, having seen it once ;
Yet here awhile remain, prisoner well pleased
Of reboant winds. Within this mountain cove
Their sound alone finds entrance. Lightly the
    waves
Rolled from the outer to the inner bay,
Dance in blue silver o'er the silver sands ;
While, like a chain-bound antelope by some child
Mocked oft with tempting hand and fruit upheld
Our quick caïque vaults up among the reeds,
The ripples that plunge past it upward sending
O'er the grey margin matted with sea-pink
Ripplings of light. The moon is veiled ; a mile
Below the mountain's eastern range it hangs ;
Yon gleam is but its reflex, from white clouds
Scattered along Parnassian peaks of snow.

III.

I see but waves and snows. Memory alone
Fruition hath of what this morn was mine :
O'er many a beauteous scene at once she broods
And feeds on joys without confusion blent
Like mingling sounds or odours. Now she rests
On that serene expanse, the confluence
Of three long vales, in sweetness upward heaved

Ample and rich as Juno's breast what time
The Thunderer's breath in sleep moves over it;
Bathes in those runnels now, that raced in light
This morn as at some festival of streams
Through arbutus and ilex, wafting each
Upon its glassy track a several breeze,
Each with its tale of joy or playful sadness.
Fair nymphs, by great Apollo's fall untouched!
Sing, sing, for ever! When did golden Phœbus
Look sad one moment for a fair nymph's fall?

IV.

A still, black glen; below, a stream-like copse
Of hoary olives; rocks like walls beside,
Never by Centaur trod though these fresh gales
Give man the Centaur's strength. Again I mount
From cliff to cliff, from height to height ascend;
Glitters Castalia's Fount; I see, I touch it!
That Rift once more I reach, the Oracular seat
Whose arching rocks half meet in air suspense;
Twixt them is one blue streak of heaven; hard by
Dim Temples hollowed in the stone, for rites
Mysterious shaped, or mansions of the dead:
Released, I turn and see, far far below,
A vale so rich in floral garniture
And odours from the orange and the sea,
So girt with white peaks flashing from sky chasms,
So lighted with the vast blue dome of Heaven,

So lulled with music from the winds and waves,
The guest of Phœbus clasps his hands and shouts,
'There is but one such spot; from Heaven Apollo
Beheld! and chose it for his earthly shrine!'

V.

Phœbus Apollo! loftiest shape of all
That glorified the range of Grecian song,
By poet hymned or shepherd when the rocks
Confessed the first bright impress of thy feet;
By many an old man praised when Thracian blasts
Sang loud and pine-wood stores began to fail;
Served by the sick man searching hill and plain
For herb assuasive; courted by sad maids
On whose pure lips thy fancied kiss descended
Softly as vernal beam on primrose cold;
By Fortune's troubled favourites ofttime sued
For dubious answer, then when Fate malign
Mounting beyond the horizon of high Hopes,
Her long fell glance had cast on them—Apollo!
Who, what wert thou? Let those that read thy
         tale
In clouded chambers of the North, reply
'An empty dream!' bid them fling far the scroll,
The dusty parchment put aside for ever,
Or scan with light from thy Parnassian skies!
For commentator's lamp give them thine orb
Flaming on high, transfixing cloud and wave

Or noontide laurel—as the Zephyr strikes it
Daphnè once more shrinks trembling from thy
   beams—
Were these but fancies? O'er the world they
   reared
The only empire verily universal
Founded by man ; for Fancy heralds Thought,
Thought Act, and nations Are as they Believe.
Strong were such fancies, strong not less than fair !
The plant spontaneous of Society
In Greece, by them with stellar power was dewed,
And, nursed by their far influence, grew and
   flowered :
A state of order and fair fellowship
Man with man walking, not in barbarous sort
His own prey finding, each, and his own God ;
A state of freedom not by outward force
Compressed or icelike knit by negatives ;
A frank communion of deep thoughts with glad
Light cares with grave ; a changeful melody
Varying each moment yet in soul the same ;
A temple raised for beauty and defence ;
An armèd dance held for a festival ;
A balanced scheme that gave each power a limit
Each toil a crown and every art her Muse !
O ! frank and graceful life of Grecian years !
Whence came thy model? From the Grecian
   heaven;

The loves and wars of Gods, their works and ways,
Their several spheres distinct yet interwreathed,
By Greece were copied on a humbler stage.
Our thoughts soar high to light our paths on earth;
Terrestrial circles from celestial take
Their impress in man's science; stars unreached
Our course o'er ocean guide; Orphean sounds
The walls of cities raised : thus mythic bards
For all the legislators legislated !

VI.

Yet these were idols : such as worshipped these
Were worshippers of idols.   Holy and True !
How many are there not idolaters ?
Traditions, Systems, Passion, Interest, Power--
Are these not idols ?   Ay, of idols worst !
Not that men worship these; but that before them
Down-bent the faculty that worship pays
Shrivels and dies.   Man's spirit alone adores,
And can adore but Spirit.   What is not God,
Howe'er our fears may crouch, or habit grovel
Or sensuous fancy dote, we worship not :
Unless God looks on man he cannot pray;
Such is Idolatry's masked Atheism !
—Yes, these were idols, for man made them such !
By a corrupt heart all things are corrupted,
God's works alike or products of the mind :
The Soul, insurgent 'gainst its Maker, lacks

The strength its vassal powers to rule. The Will
To blind caprice grows subject; Reason, torn
From Faith, becomes the Understanding's slave;
And Passion's self in appetite is lost.
Then Idols dominate—despots by Self-will
Set up where Law and Faith alike are dead,
To awe the anarchy of godless souls.
Nought but a Worship spiritual and pure,
Profound, habitual, strong through loving awe,
A true heart's tribute to the God of Truth,
From selfishness redeemed, and so from sense
Secured, though conversant with shapes of sense,
Nought but such Worship with spontaneous
    force
From our whole Being equably ascending
As odour from a flower or fount's clear breath,
Redeems us from Idolatry. In vain
Are proudly wise appeals that deprecate
Rites superstitious; vain are words though shrill
With scorn; stark pointed finger; forehead ridged
With blear-eyed Scepticism's myriad wrinkles:
Saintly we must be or Idolatrous.
After his image Man creates him Gods,
Kneading the symbol—as a symbol pure
And salutary—to a form compact
With servile soul and mean mechanic hand:
Thus to their native dust his Thoughts return,
Abashed, and of mortality convinced.

I

VII.

At Salem was the Law. The Holy Land
Its orient terrace by the ocean reared
And thereon walked the Holy One, at cool
Of the world's morn; there visible state He kept:
At Salem was the Law on stone inscribed;
But over all the world, within man's heart
The unwritten Law abode, from earliest time
Upon our being stampt, nor wholly lost:
Men saw it, loved it, praised—and disobeyed.
Therefore the Conscience, whose applausive voice
Their march triumphant should have led with joy
To all perfection, from a desert pealed
The Baptist's note alone—' Repent, repent;'
And men with song more flattering filled their ears.
Yet still the undersong was holy! long—
Though cast on days unblest, though sin-defiled—
The mind accepted, yea the heart revered,
That which the Will lacked strength to follow.
   Conscience,
Her crown monarchal first, her fillet next
Snatched from her sacred brows, a minstrel's
   wreath
Assumed, and breathed in song her soul abroad:
On outcast Duty's grave she with her tears
Dropt flowers funereal of surpassing beauty,
With Reason walked, the right path indicated,
Though her imperative voice was heard no more;

Nor spake in vain. Man—fallen man—was great,
Remembering ancient greatness : Hymn and tale
Held, each, some portion of dismembered Truth,
Severely sung by poets wise and brave.
They sang of Justice, God's great Attribute,
With tragic buskin and a larger stride
Following the fated victim step by step :
They sang of Love crowning the toils of life:
Of Joy they sang ; for Joy, that gift divine,
Primal and wingèd creature, with full breath
Through all the elastic limbs of Grecian fable
Poured her redundant life, the noble tongue
Strong as the brazen clang of ringing arms
With resonance of liquid sounds enriching
Sweet as the music-laughter of the Gods :
Of heavenly Pity, Prophet-like they sang ;
And, feeling after good though finding not,
Of Him that Good not yet in Flesh revealed
By ceaseless vigils, tears, and lifted palms,
And yearnings infinite and unrepressed,
A separate and authentic witness bore.
Thus was the end foreshown ; thus Error's 'cloud
Turned forth its silver lining on the night.'
Thus too—for us at least a precious gift,
Dear for the lore it grasped, by all it lacked
Sternly made bold vainglorious thoughts to
    chide,—
Wisdom shone forth ; but not for men unwise :

Her beams but taint the dead ; man's Guilt and
    Woe
She proved, and her own Helplessness confessed.
Such were her two great functions. Woe to those
Who live with Art for Faith, and Bards for Priests !
These are supplanted : Sense their loftiest hopes
Will sap ; and fiends usurp their oracles !

VIII.

Olympian dreams, farewell ! your spell is past ;
I turn from you away ; from Eros' self,
From heavenly Beauty on thy crystal brow
Uranian Venus, starred in gentlest light,
From thee, Prometheus chained on Caucasus,
Io from thee, sad wanderer o'er the earth,
From thee, great Hercules, the son of Heaven
And of Humanity held long in pain ;
Heroic among men, by labours tried,
Descending to the Shades and leading thence
The Lost ; while infant still, a Serpent-slayer;
In death a dread and mystic Sacrifice :
From thee more high than all, from thee, Apollo !
Light of the world whose sacred beam, like words,
Illustrated the forehead of the earth,
Supreme of Harmonists, whose song flowed forth
Pure from that light ; great slayer of the Serpent
That mocked thy Mother ; master of that craft
Helpful to anguished flesh ; Oracular :

Secretly speaking wisdom to the just ;
Openly to the lost from lips despised
Like thy Cassandra's flinging it to waste :—
Phœbus Apollo ! here at thy chief shrine
From thee I turn ; and stern confession make
That not the vilest weed yon ripple casts
Here at my feet, but holds a loftier gift
Than all the Grecian Legends ! Let them go—
Because the mind of man they lifted up,
But corruptible instincts left to grovel
On Nature's common plane, yea and below it ;
Because they slightly healed the People's wound,
And sought in genial fancy, finite hopes,
Proportioned life and dialectic art,
A substitute for Virtue ; and because
They gave for nothing that which Faith should
    earn,
Casting the pearls of Truth 'neath bestial feet ;
Because they washed the outside of the cup,
And dropped a thin veil o'er the face of Death ;
Because they neither brought man to his God,
Nor let him feel his weakness— let them go !
Wisdom that raises not her sons is folly :
Truth in its unity alone is Truth.

IX.

What now is Delphi? Where that temple now
Dreadful to kings ; with votive offering stored

·Tripod, or golden throne from furthest lands,
Or ingot huge ?   Where now that tremulous stone,
Centre of all things deemed—Earth's beating heart?
What now is Delphi? yea, or Hellas' self,
With all her various States ; epitome
Of Nations ; stage whereon in little space
Forecasting Time rehearsed his thousand parts ?
Sparta's one camp ; the sacred plain of Thebes,
That plain pious as rich whence grateful Ceres
The hand that blesses Earth upraised to Heaven ;
The unboastful freedom of Arcadian vales ;
Athens with Academic Arts, and ships
Far seen from pillared headlands ?   Where, O
    where
Olympia's chariot-course that bent the eyes
Of Greece on one small ring shining like fire ;
Or they, that sacred Council, at whose nod
King and Republic trembled ?   Gone for ever !
Vine on the wave diffused budding with Isles ;
Bower of young Earth, wherein the East and West,
Wedded, their beauteous progeny upreared ;
Hellas, by Nature blest, by Freedom nursed,
By Providence led on through discipline
Of change, till that Philosophy was formed
Which made one City man's perpetual Teacher—
Hellas is past.   A lamentable voice
Forth from the caverns of Antiquity
Issuing in mystery, answers, Where is Egypt ?

Egypt of magic craft and starry lore,
Eternal brooder on the unknown past
Through the long vista of her Kings and Priests
Descried, as setting Moon beyond the length
Of forest aisle or desert colonnade ;
Eldest of Nations, and apart, like Night
Dark veiled amid the synod of the Gods ?
The sun and stars, above her circling stare
At pyramids sand-drowned, and long processions
Now petrified to lines of marble shapes
That lead to Sphinx-girt Cities of the Dead !
Where now is Babylon, mighty by peace
And gold, and men countless as forest leaves ?
Persia, the Macedonian, Carthage, Tyre ?
All gone—restored to earth ! Great Rome herself,
Haughty with arcs of triumph, theatres
Sphered to embrace all nations and their Gods,
Roads from one centre piercing lands remote,
Bridges, fit type of conquest's giant stride—
Great Rome herself, empire of War and Law,
Yoking far regions, harrowing those fields
Reserved for Christian seed—Great Rome herself
Was, and is not ! The eternal edict stands :
That power from God which comes not, drops and
  dies.

X.

Hark to that sound ! yon ocean Eagle drives
The mist of morn before her, seaward launched

From her loved nest on Delphi. She, though stern,
Can love—a divine instinct, that outlasts,
Phœbus, thy fabulous honours ! Far away
The storms are dying ; and the night-bird pours
Encouraged thus, her swift and rapturous song.
Ah ! when that song is over I depart !
Return, my wandering thoughts ! the ascended Moon
Smiles on her Brother's peaks, and many a ridge
Her glance solicits, many a stirring wood
Exults in her strong radiance as she glides
On from the pine gulf to the gulf of clouds.
Return, my thoughts ! the innumerous cedar cones
Of Lebanon must lull you now no more ;
Nor fall of Empires with as soft a sound.
O'er famed Colonos stoop no more in trance
Eyeing the city towers. No longer muse
With mind divided though a single heart,
On legend—true or erring ! Earth can yield
No scene more fair than this ; and Nature's beauty
Is ever irreproachable. Return !
A long breath take of this ambrosial clime
Ere lost the sweetness : sigh, yet be content :
Fill here your golden urns ; be fresh for ever !

SONNETS.

FLOWERS I would bring if flowers could make
    thee fairer
And music if the Muse were dear to thee,
For loving these would make thee love the bearer;
But sweetest songs forget their melody,
And loveliest flowers would but conceal the
    wearer :—
A rose I marked, and might have plucked; but
    she
Blushed as she bent, imploring me to spare her,
Nor spoil her beauty by such rivalry.
Alas! and with what gifts shall I pursue thee,
What offerings bring, what treasures lay before
    thee;
When earth with all her floral train doth woo thee
And all old poets and old songs adore thee,
And love to thee is naught; from passionate mood
Secured by joy's complacent plenitude!

SHE whom this heart must ever hold most dear,
This heart in happy bondage held so long,
Began to sing: At first a gentle fear
Rosied her countenance, for she is young,

And he who loves her most of all was near;
But, when at last her voice grew full and strong,
O! from their ambush sweet, how rich and clear
Leaped the bright notes abroad—a rapturous
    throng!
Her little hands were sometimes flung apart,
And sometimes palm to palm together prest;
While wave-like blushes rising from her breast
Kept time with that aërial melody;
A music to the sight!—I standing nigh
Received the falling fountain in my heart.

The happiest lovers that in verse have writ,
After all vows to perfect beauty paid,
Full oft their hymns of triumph intermit
And harp and brow with funeral chaplets shade;
A Babylonian choir on earth they sit
In garb of exiles; sadly they upbraid
Beauty and Joy that only bloom to fade,
And Love and Hope to Death and Ruin knit.
What shall we say? Have poets never loved?
For small that love which fears that love can die—
Have those that earthly immortality
Award, the name itself a mockery proved?
Or of the Spirit of Life so full are they
That with Death's shadow they are pleased to
    play?

INCOMPATIBILITY.

FORGIVE me that I love you as I do,
Friend patient long ; too patient to reprove
The inconvenience of superfluous love :
You feel that it molests you, and 'tis true.
In a light bark you sit, with a full crew.
Your life full orbed, compelled strange love to meet,
Becomes, by such addition, incomplete :—
Because I love I leave you. O adieu !
Perhaps when I am gone the thought of me
May sometimes be your acceptable guest.
Indeed you love me : but my company
Old time makes tedious ; and to part is best.
Not without Nature's will are natures wed :—
O gentle Death, how dear thou mak'st the dead !

HUMAN LIFE.

SAD is our youth, for it is ever going,
Crumbling away beneath our very feet ;
Sad is our life, for onward it is flowing,
In current unperceived because so fleet ;
Sad are our hopes, for they were rich in sowing,
But tares, self sown, have overtopped the wheat ;
Sad are our joys, for they were sweet in blowing,
And still, O still, their dying breath is sweet :

And sweet is youth, although it hath bereft us
Of that which made our childhood sweeter still;
And sweet our life's decline, for it hath left us
A nearer Good to cure an older Ill;
And sweet are all things, when we learn to prize them
Not for their sake, but His who grants them or denies them.

THE SUN GOD.

I saw the Master of the Sun. He stood
High in his luminous car, himself more bright;
An Archer of immeasurable might:
On his left shoulder hung his quivered load;
Spurned by his steeds the eastern mountain glowed;
Forward his eager eye, and brow of light
He bent; and, while both hands that arch embowed,
Shaft after shaft pursued the flying Night.
No wings profaned that godlike form: around
His neck high held an ever-moving crowd
Of locks hung glistening: while such perfect sound
Fell from his bowstring, that th' ethereal dome
Thrilled as a dewdrop; and each passing cloud
Expanded, whitening like the ocean foam.

URANIA.

URANIA ! Voice of Heaven, sidereal Muse !
Lo, through the dark vault issuing from afar
She comes, reclining on a lucid star :
Her large eyes, trembling through celestial dews,
The glory of high thoughts far off diffuse ;
While the bright surges of her refluent hair
Stream back, upraised upon sustaining air
Which lifts that scarf deep-dyed in midnight hues
To a wide arch above her hung like heaven.
I closed my eyes. Athwart me, like a blast,
Music as though of jubilant gods was driven.
Once more I gazed. That form divine had passed
Earth's dark confine. The ocean's utmost rim
Burned yet a moment : then the world grew dim.

THE POETRY OF LIFE.

DIAN ! thy brother of the golden beams
Is hailed for ever as the Lord of Song,
Master of manly verse and mystic dreams :
Doth, then, no female lyre to thee belong ?
Say, is that silver bow whose crescent gleams,
Above black pinewoods lifted, or low-hung
'Twixt hornèd rocks, or troubling midnight streams,
With immelodious chord, and silent, strung ?

Ah no, not so ! Thou too art musical !
The world is full of poetry unwrit ;
Dew-woven nets that virgin hearts enthrall,
Darts of glad thought through infant brains that flit,
Hope and pursuit, loved bonds and fancies free ;—
Poor were our earth of these bereft and thee !

SORROW.

COUNT each affliction, whether light or grave,
God's messenger sent down to thee ; do thou
With courtesy receive him ; rise and bow ;
And, ere his shadow pass thy threshold, crave
Permission first his heavenly feet to lave ;
Then lay before him all thou hast : allow
No cloud of passion to usurp thy brow,
Or mar thy hospitality ; no wave
Of mortal tumult to obliterate
The soul's marmoreal calmness : Grief should be,
Like joy, majestic, equable, sedate ;
Confirming, cleansing, raising, making free ;
Strong to consume small troubles ; to commend
Great thoughts, grave thoughts, thoughts lasting to the end.

NATIONAL APOSTASY.

TRAMPLING a dark hill, a red sun athwart,
I saw a host that rent their clothes and hair,
And dashed their spread hands 'gainst that sunset
    glare,
And cried, 'Go from us, God, since God thou art!
Utterly from our coasts and towns depart,
Court, camp, and senate-hall, and mountain bare;
Our pomp Thou troublest and our feast dost
    scare,
And with Thy temples dost confuse our mart!
Depart Thou from our hearing and our seeing:
Depart Thou from the works and ways of men;
Their laws, their thoughts, the inmost of their
    being:
Black Nightmare, hence! that earth may breathe
    again.'
'Can God depart?' I asked. A voice replied
Close by, 'Not so; each Sin at heart is *Deicide.*'

UNIVERSAL HISTORY.

METHOUGHT I gazed upon a dusky Round,
Our mortal planet's monumental urn;
Around its orb with many a spiral turn
Ascending, a Procession slowly wound.

There saw I laurelled poets, kings renowned;
Prophets I saw from earth's remotest bourne:
There saw I maids and youths, old men forlorn,
And conquerors full-armed, and captives bound.
A Funeral pomp methought it seemed far down
In pale relief; and, side by side, therein
Hooded, there paced, a Sorrow and a Sin:
Midway in ampler ring, and vision clear,
A Sacrifice embraced that mighty sphere:
Above, a lovely Bridal was its crown.

TROILUS AND CRESSIDA.

HAD I been worthy of the love you gave,
That love withdrawn had left me sad but strong;
My heart had been as silent as my tongue,
My bed had been unfevered as my grave;
I had not striven for what I could not save;
Back, back to heaven my great hopes I had flung;
To have much suffered, having done no wrong,
Had seemed to me that noble part the brave
Account it ever. What this hour I am
Affirms the unworthiness that in me lurked:
Some sapping poison through my substance worked,
Some sin not trivial, though it lacked a name,

Which ratifies the deed that you have done
With plain approval. Other plea seek none.

FOR we the mighty mountain plains have trod
Both in the glow of sunset and sunrise ;
And lighted by the moon of southern skies :
The snow-white torrent of the thundering flood
We two have watched together : In the wood
We two have felt the warm tears dim our eyes
While zephyrs softer than an infant's sighs
Ruffled the light air of our solitude.
O Earth, maternal Earth, and thou O Heaven,
And Night first born, who now, e'en now, dost
    waken
The host of stars, thy constellated train,
Tell me if those can ever be forgiven,
Those abject, who together have partaken
These Sacraments of Nature—and in vain ?

HAPPY are they who kiss thee morn and even
Parting the hair upon thy forehead white ;
For them the sky is bluer and more bright
And purer their thanksgivings rise to Heaven :
Happy are they to whom thy songs are given ;
Happy are they on whom thy hands alight ;
And happiest they for whom thy prayers at night
In tender piety so oft have striven.

Away with vain regrets and selfish sighs!
Even I, dear friend, am lonely, not unblest,
Permitted sometimes on that form to gaze,
Or feel the light of those consoling eyes—
If but a moment on my cheek it stays
I know that gentle beam from all the rest!

THE spring of my sweet life thou madest thine,
And on my summer glories thou hast fed;
And now the vernal melodies are dead
On lips that mourn for joys no longer mine;
The summer brilliance now hath ceased to shine
Upon a brow so oft disquieted
By agonising doubts: thy love is fled;
And thou art flying—how dare I repine?
How could I hope so great a love would cleave
To one whose fault too well was known to thee?
Lament not, O my friend, or if thou grieve
For me lament not though my grief thou share,
For I have known in dreams my destiny,
And what I ought to welcome I can bear.

ROBERT BROWNING.

I.

Gone from us! that sweet singer of late days—
Sweet singer should be strong—who tarrying here,
Chose still rough music for his themes austere,
Hard-headed, aye, but tender-hearted lays,
Carefully careless, garden half, half maze.
His thoughts he sang, deep thoughts to thinkers dear,
Now flashing under gleam of smile or tear,
Now veiled in language like a breezy haze
Chance-pierced by sunbeams from the lake it covers.
He sang man's ways—not heights of sage or saint,
Not highways broad, not haunts endeared to lovers:
He sang life's bye-ways, sang its angles quaint,
Its Runic lore inscribed on stave or stone,
Song's short-hand strain—its key oft his alone.

II.

Shakespeare's old oak "gnarled and unwedgeable"
Yields not so sweet a wood to harp or lyre
As tree of smoother grain; and chorded shell
Is spanned by strings tenderer than iron wire.
What then? Stern tasks iron and oak require!
Iron deep-mined, hard oak from stormy fell:
Steel-armed the black ship breasts the ocean's swell
Oak-ribbed laughs back the raging tempest's ire.

Old friend, thy song I deem a ship whose hold
Is stored with mental spoils of ampler price
Than Spain's huge galleons in her age of gold,
Or Indian carracks from the isles of spice.
Brave Argosy ! cleave long the waves as now,
And all the sea-gods sing around thy prow !
   January, 1890.

A WINTER NIGHT IN THE WOODS.

WHEN first the Spring her glimmering chaplets wove
This way and that way 'mid the boughs high hung
We watched the hourly work, while thrushes sung
A song that shook with joy their bowered alcove :
Summer came next ; she roofed with green the grove,
And deepening shades to flower-sweet alleys clung :
Then last—one dirge from many a golden tongue—
The chiding leaves with chiding Autumn strove.
These were but Nature's preludes.   Last is first !
Winter, uplifting high both flail and fan,
With the great forests dealt as Death with man ;
And therefore through their desolate roofs hath burst
This splendour veiled no more by earthly bars ;
Infinite Heaven, and the fire-breathing stars !

MEMORIAL.

I.

Alone among thy books once more I sit;
No sound there stirs except the flapping fire:
Strange shadows of old times about me flit
As sinks the midnight lamp or flickers higher.
I see thee pace the room; with eye thought-lit
Back, back thou com'st once more to my desire:
Low-toned thou read'st once more the verse new
    writ,
Too deep, too pure for worldlings to admire.
That brow all honour, that all-gracious hand,
That cordial smile and clear voice musical,
That noble bearing, mien of high command
Yet void of pride—to-night I have them all.
Ah, phantoms vain of thought! The Christmas air
Is white with flying flakes. Where art thou—where?

II.

To-night upon thy roof the snows are lying,
The Christmas snows lie heavy on thy trees,
A dying dirge that soothes the year in dying
Swells from the woodlands on the midnight breeze.
Our loss is ancient; many a heart is sighing
This night, a late one, or by slow degrees
Heals some old wound, to God's high grace
    replying—
A time there was when thou wert like to these.

Where art thou? In what unimagined sphere
Liv'st thou, sojourner, or no transient guest?
By whom companioned? Access hath she near,
In life thy nearest and beloved the best?
What memory hast thou of thy loved ones here?
Hangs the great Vision o'er thy place of rest?

III.

'Sweet-sounding bells, blithe summoners to prayer!'
The answer man can yield not ye bestow;
Your answer is a little Infant bare
Wafted to earth on night winds whispering low.
Blow him to Bethlehem, airs angelic, blow!
There doth the Mother-maid his couch prepare:
His harbour is her bosom! Drop him there
Soft as a snowflake on a bank of snow.
Sole Hope of man! sole Hope for us, for Thee!
'To us a Prince is given; a Child is born!'—
Thou sang'st of Bethlehem and of Calvary,
The Maid Immaculate and the twisted Thorn:
Where'er thou art, not far, not far is He
Whose banner whitens in yon Christmas morn!

1860.

THE BATTLE OF CLONTARF:

OR, THE KING'S SACRIFICE.

THE battle of Clontarf, fought A.D. 1014, annulled for ever the Danish power in Ireland. During two centuries and more the sons of the North had landed on the Irish coasts, sacked the monasteries, burned the cities and churches, and in many places well-nigh destroyed the Christian civilisation of earlier times, although they were never able to establish a monarchy throughout Ireland. The native dynasties for the most part remained; and Brian the Great, then King of all Ireland, though aged and blind, led forth the native hosts against the invaders for one supreme effort. He placed his son Murrough in command; and he offered up his life for his country and wrought her deliverance. His sons and his grandson partook his glory and his fate. His death was a favourite theme with the chroniclers and bards of ancient Erin.

I.

'ANSWER, thou that from the height
Look'st to left, and look'st to right,
Answer thou, how goes the fight?'

II.

Thus spake King Brian, by his tent
Kneeling, with sceptred hands that leant
Upon that altar which, where'er
He marched, kept pure his path with prayer:
For, after all his triumphs past
  That made him wondrous 'mid his peers,
On the blind King God's will had cast
  The burden of his fourscore years:

And therefore when that morn, at nine,
　　He rode along the battle's van
No sword he lifted, but the Sign
　　Of Him who died for man.
King Brian's fleshly strength decayed,
　　Three times in puissance waxed his spirit,
　　And tall, like oak-trees, towered his merit.
And like a praying host he prayed.
From nine to twelve, with crown on head,
Full fifty prayers the King had said;
And unto each such power was given
It shook the unopening gates of heaven.

III.

'O King, the battle goes this hour
　　As when two seas are met in might,
When billow billow doth devour,
　　And tide with tide doth fight:

'I watch the waves of war; but none
　　Can see what banners rise or fall:
Sea-clouds on rush, sea-crests on run,
　　And blood is over all.'

IV.

Then prayed the King once more, head-bare,
And made himself a cross in prayer,
With outstretched arms and forehead prone
Staid on that topmost altar-stone

Gem-charged, and cleansed from mortal taint,
And strong with bones of many a Saint.
In youth his heart for God had yearned
And Eire : now thrice his youth returned :
A child full oft, ere woke the bird,
The convent's nocturns he had heard
In old Kincora, or that isle
Which guards, thus late, its wasted pile,
While winds of night the tall towers shook ;
And he would peer into that Book
Which lay, lamp-lit, on eagle's wings,
 Wherein God's Saints in gold and blue
Stood up, and Prophets stood, and Kings ;
 And he the Martyrs knew,
And maids, and confessors each one,
 And—tabernacled there in light—
That blissful Virgin enough bright
To light a burnt-out sun.
The blazoned Letters well he kenned
 That stood like gateways keeping ward,
 Before the Feast-Days set to guard
Long ways of wisdom without end :
He knew the music notes black-barred,
 And music notes, like planted spears
Whereon who bends a fixed regard
 The gathering anthem hears
Like wakening storms 'mid pines that lean
Ere sunrise o'er some dusk ravine.

The thoughts that nursed his youth, that hour
Were with his age, and armed with power.

V.

So fifty Psalms he sang, and then
Rolled round his sightless eyes again
And spake; 'Thou watcher on the height,
Make answer quick, how goes the fight?'

VI.

' O King, the battle goes as when
    The mill-wheel circles round and round:
The battle reels; and bones of men
    Beneath its wheel are ground:

' The war-field lies like Tomar's wood
    By axes marred, or charred with fire
Where, black o'er wood-ways ruin-strewed,
    Rises the last oak spire.'

VII.

Then to his altar by the tent
Once more King Brian turned, and bent
Unsceptred hands and head discrowned
Down from that altar to the ground
In such sort that the cold March air
With fir-cones swept his snow-white hair,

And prayed, 'O Thou that from the skies
  Dost see what is, and what must be,
Make mine and me Thy Sacrifice
  But set this People free!'

VIII.

That hour, he knew, in many a fane
Late ravaged by the Pagan Dane
  God's priests were offering, far and wide,
  The Mass of the Presanctified;
For lo! it was Good Friday morn,
And Christ once more was crowned with thorn:
God's Church, he knew, from niche and shrine
  Had swept those gauds that time consumes,
Whate'er sea-cave, or wood, or mine
  Yield from their sunless wombs:
Veiled were the sacred images,
He knew, like vapour-shrouded trees;
Vanished gold lamp, and chalice rare;
The astonished altars stripped and bare
Because upon the cross, stone-dead,
Christ lay that hour disraimented.

IX.

He prayed—then spake—'How goes the fight?'
Then answer reached him from the height:—

X.

'O King, the battle goes as though
　　God weighed two nations in His scale;
And now the fates of Eire sink low,
　　Now theirs that wear the mail:

'O King, thy sons, through God's decree,
　　Are dead—save one, the best of all,
Murrough—and now, ah woe is me!
　　I see his standard fall!'

XI.

It fell: but as it fell, above
Through lightning-lighted skies on drove
A thousand heavenly standards, dyed
In martyrdom's ensanguined tide;
And every tower, and town, and fane
　　That blazed of old round Erin's shore
Down crashed, it seemed, in heaven again,
　　So dire that thunder's roar!
The wrath had come: the Danes gave way;
For Brian's prayer had power that day;
Seaward they rushed, the race abhorred—
The sword of prayer had quelled their sword:
So fled they to the ship-thronged coast;
　　But, random-borne through Tolga's glade,
A remnant from that routed host
　　Rushed by where Brian prayed

And, swinging forth his brand, down leaped
    Black Brodar, he that foremost rode,
And from the kingly shoulders swept
    The old head, praising God ;
And cried aloud, 'Let all men tell
That Brodar, he that leagues with Hell,
That Brodar of the magic mail
Slew Brian of the Gael.'

XII.

Him God destroyed ! The Accursed One lay
    Like beast, unburied where he fell :
But Brian and his sons this day
    In Armagh Church sleep well.
And Brian's grandson strong and fair,
Clutching a Sea-King by the hair,
Went with him far through Tolga's wave,
Went with him to the same sea-grave.
So Eire gave thanks to God, though sad,
    And took the blessing and the bale,
And sang, in funeral garments clad,
    The vengeance of the Gael.
Silent all night the Northmen haled
    Their dead adown the bleeding wharf :—
Far north at dawn the Pirates sailed ;
    But on thy shore, Clontarf,
Old Eire once more with wan cheeks wet
    Gave thanks that He who shakes the skies

Had burst His people's bond, and yet
    Decreed that Sacrifice :
For God is One Who gives and takes,
    Who lifts the low, and fells the proud ;
Who loves His land of Eire, and makes
    His rainbow in His cloud.

Thus sang to Eire her Bard of old ;
    Thus sang to trampled kerne and serf,
While, sunset-like, her age of gold
    Came back to green Clontarf.

THE THREE STATES OF WOMANHOOD.

(FROM 'HOW SAINT CUTHBERT KEPT HIS PENTECOST AT CARLISLE.')

                      Next, to Cuthbert drew
Three maidens hand in hand, lovely as Truth,
Trustful, though shy : their thoughts, when hidden
    most,
Wore but a semilucid veil as when
Through gold-touched crystal of the lime new-
    leaved
On April morns the symmetry looks forth
Of branch and bough distinct. Smiling, they put
At last their question : 'Tell us man of God

What life, of lives that women lead, is best ;
Then show us forth in parables that life !'
 He answered : ' Three ; for each of these is
  best :
First comes the Maiden's : she who lives it well
Serves God in marble chapel white as snow,
His priestess—His alone. Cold flowers each morn
She culls ere sunrise by the stainless stream
And lays them on that chapel's altar-stone,
And sings her matins there. Her feet are swift
All day in labours 'mid the vales below
Cheering sad hearts : each evening she returns
To that high fane and there her vespers sings ;
Then sleeps, and dreams of heaven.'
        With witching smile
The youngest of that beauteous triad cried :
' That life is sweetest ! I would be that maid !'
Cuthbert resumed : ' The Christian Wife comes
  next :
She drinks a deeper draught of life : round her
In ampler sweep its sympathies extend :
An infant's cry has knocked against her heart
Evoking thence that human love wherein
Self-love hath least. Through infant eyes a Spirit
Hath looked upon her, crying, "I am thine !
Creature from God—dependent yet on thee ! "
Thenceforth she knows how greatness blends with
  weakness ;

Reverence, thenceforth with pity linked, reveals
To her the pathos of the life of man
A thing divine, and yet at every pore
Bleeding from crownèd brows. A heart thus large
Hath room for many sorrows. What of that?
Its sorrow is its dowry's noblest part.
She bears it not alone. Such griefs, so shared—
Sickness, and fear, and vigils lone and long,
Waken her heart to love sublimer far
Than ecstasies of youth could comprehend ;
Lift her at times to heights serene as those
The Ascetic treadeth.'
     'I would be that wife!'
Thus cried the second of those maidens three :
Yet who that gazed upon her could have guessed
Creature so soft could bear a heart so brave ?
She seemed that goodness which was beauteous too ;
Virtue at once and Virtue's bright reward ;
Delight that lifts, not lowers us ; made for heaven ;—
Made too to change to heaven some brave man's hearth.
She added thus : 'Of lives that women lead
Tell us the third!'
    Gently the Saint replied :
'The third is Widowhood—a wintry sound ;

And yet, for her who widow is indeed
That winter something keeps of autumn's gold,
Something regains of Spring's first-flower snow-
    white
Snow-cold, and colder for its rim of green.
She feels no more the warmly greeting hand ;
The eyes she brightened rest on her no more ;
Her full-orbed being now is cleft in twain :
Her past is dead : daily from memory's self
Dear things depart ; yet still she is a wife,
A wife the more because of bridal bonds
Lives but their essence waiting wings in heaven ;—
More wife, and yet, in that great loneliness
More maiden too than when first maidenhood
Lacked what it missed not. Like that other
    maid
She too a lonely priestess serves her God ;
Yea, though her chapel be a funeral vault,
Its altar black like Death, the flowers thereon
Tinct with the Blood Divine. Above that vault
She hears the anthems of the Spouse of Christ,
Widowed, like her, though Bride.'

            ' O fair, O sweet,
O beauteous lives all three ; fair lot of women ! '
Thus cried again the youngest of those Three,
Too young to know the touch of grief—or cause
    it—
A plant too lightly-leaved to cast a shade.

K

The eldest with pale cheek and lids tear-wet
Made answer sad : 'I would not be a widow.'
    Then Cuthbert spake once more with smile
        benign :
'I said that each of these three lives is best :—
There are who live those three conjoined in one :
The nun thus lives. What maid is maid like her
Who, free to choose, has vowed a maidenhood
Secure 'gainst chance or choice? What bride like
    her
Whose Bridegroom is the spouse of vestal Souls?
What widow lives in such austere retreat,
Such hourly thought of him she ne'er can join
Save through the gate of death? If those three
    lives
In separation lived are fair and sweet,
How show they, blent in one?'
                      Of those who heard
The most part gladdened ; those who knew how
    high
Virtue, renouncing all besides for God,
Hath leave to soar on earth. Yet many sighed,
Jealous for happy homesteads. Cuthbert marked
That shame-faced sadness, and continued thus :
'To praise the nun reproaches not, O friends,
But praises best that life of hearth and home
At Cana blessed by Him who shared it not.
The uncloistered life is holy too, and oft

Through changeful years in soft succession links
Those three fair types of woman ; holds, diffused,
That excellence severe which Life Detached
Sustains in concentration.' Long he mused ;
Then added thus : ' When last I roved these vales
There lived, not distant far, a blessed one
Revered by all : her name was Ethelreda :
I knew her long, and much from her I learned.
Beneath her Pagan father's roof there sat
Ofttimes a Christian youth. With him the child
Walked, calling him " her friend." He loved the
    maid :
Still young he drew her to the fold of Christ ;
Espoused her three years later ; died in war
Ere three months passed. For her he never died !
Immortalised by faith that bond lived on ;
And now close by, and now 'mid Saints of heaven
She saw her husband walk. She never wept ;
That fire which lit her eye and flushed her cheek
Dried up, it seemed, her tears : the neighbours
    round
Called her " the lady of the happy marriage."
She died long since, I doubt not.' Forward
    stepped
A slight, pale maid, the daughter of a bard,
And answered thus : ' Two months ago she died.'
Then Cuthbert : ' Tell me, maiden, of her death :
And see you be not chary of your words,

For well I loved that woman.'   Tears unfelt
Fast streaming down her pallid cheek, the maid
Replied, yet often paused : ' A sad, sweet end !
A long night's pain had left her living still :
I found her on the threshold of her door :—
Her cheek was white ; but, trembling round her lips
And dimly o'er her countenance spread, there lay
Something that, held in check by feebleness,
Yet tended to a smile.   A cloak tight-drawn
From the cold March wind screened her, save one hand
Stretched on her knee, that reached to where a beam,
Thin slip of watery sunshine, sunset's last,
Slid through the branches.   On that beam, methought,
Rested her eyes, half-closed.   It was not so :
For when I knelt and kissed that hand ill-warmed
Smiling she said : " The small, unwedded maid
Has missed her mark !   You should have kissed the ring !
Full forty years upon a widowed hand
It holds its own.   It takes its latest sunshine."
She lived through all that night, and died while dawned
Through snows Saint Joseph's morn.'

THE COMBAT AT THE FORD.

(FROM "THE FORAY OF QUEEN MEAVE."—THE
EARLIEST SPECIMEN OF THE IRISH EPIC.)

ARGUMENT.

QUEEN MEAVE sends her herald to Ferdīa the Firbolg,
requiring him to engage with Cuchullain in single combat.
Ferdīa refuses to fight against his ancient friend: yet,
later, he attends a royal banquet given in his honour; and
there, being drawn aside through the witcheries of the
Princess Finobar, he consents to the fight. The charioteer
of Ferdīa sees Cuchullain advancing in his war-car to the
Ford, and, rapt by a prophetic spirit, sings his triumph.
For two days the ancient friends contend against each
other with reluctance and remorse; but on the third day
the battle-rage bursts fully forth: and on the fourth,
Cuchullain, himself pierced through with wounds innumerable, slays Ferdīa by the Gae-Bulg. He lays his friend
upon the bank, at its northern side, and, standing beside
him, sings his dirge.

MEANTIME, that night within his forest lair
In dreams Cuchullain lay, and saw in dreams
Not recent fights, but ocean and that isle
Where with Ferdīa he had dwelt in youth
With Scatha—and another. And in dream
He mused ; ' The dearest of my friends survives :
These wars will pass ; Ferdīa then and I
Thenceforth are one for aye!' That self-same
    hour
The Firbolg slowly woke from troubled sleep,
Murmuring, as one in trance, ' Against my friend !
Against my only friend !' With gloomy brows
His clansmen watched him arming. One sole man

They feared; that man Cuchullain. Morn the
    while
Was dawning, though she raised nor glowing cheek
Nor ardent eyes, with silver wand not gold
Striking the unkindling portals of the East;
And, ere the sun had risen, Ferdīa bathed
Three times his forehead in the frosty stream;
And bade his charioteer attend; and drave
Begirt by stateliest equipage of war
Down to the river's brim. In regal pomp
The host confederate followed, keen to watch
With Meave, and Ailill, and with Finobar
All passions of a fight unmatched till then
On warfields of the immemorial world;
While clustered here and there on rock or mound
Minstrel and food-purveyor groom and leech
With healing herbs, and charms.
                                  The sun arose
And smote the forest-roof dew-saturate
As onward dashed through woodlands to the Ford
Cuchullain's war-car. Nearer soon it rolled
Crushing the rocks. Above those wondrous steeds
That Great One glittered through low mist of
    morn,
Splendour gloom-veiled. Ferdīa's charioteer
Half heard, half saw him. Spirit-rapt, yet awed,
Perforce thus sang he standing near the marge.
    'I hear the on-rushing of the Car! I see

There throned that warrior not of mortal mould
Swathed in the morning. Dreadful are his wheels ;
Dreadful as breaker arched, when on its crest
Stands Fear, and Fate upon the rock-strewn shore ;
But not sea-rocks they crush, those brazen wheels,
But realms, and peoples, and the necks of men.
  'I see the War-Car ! Terrible it comes,
Four-peaked ; and o'er those peaks a shadowy pall
Pavilioning dim crypt and cave of death :
I see it by the gleam of spears high held,
The glare of circling Spirits. Lo ! the same
I saw far northward drifting, months gone by,
Ere yet that madness quelled the northern land.'
  Then cried Ferdia, stationed where huge trees
Shut out unwelcome vision : ' For a bribe
Thou seest these portents, singing of my death !'
  Once more, in agony prophetic, he—
'The man within that car is Uladh's Hound !
What hound ? No stag-hound of the storm-swept
    hills :
No watch-hound watching by a merchant's store :
The hound he is that tracks the steps of Doom ;
The hound of realms o'er-run, and hosts that fly ;
The hound that laps the blood !'
                    Again he sang ;
' The Hound of Uladh is a hound with wings ;
A hound man-headed ! Yea, and o'er that head
Victory and empire, like two eagles paired

Sail onward, tempest-pinioned. Endless morn
Before him fleeting far o'er seas and lands
With shaft retorted lights his chariot-beam.
That chariot stays not; turns not: on it comes,
Like torrent shooting from a tall cliff's brow,
Level long time; then downward borne!'
                                    'A bribe!'
Once more Ferdīa cried; 'A bribe! a lie!
Traitor! for Ailill's gold and gold of Meave
Thou sing'st thy master's death-song!'
                                    By the stream
Cuchullain stood: not yet he knew his foe;
That foe who slowly to the Ford advanced
Full panoplied, and in his hand a spear.
Long gazed they each on each. Cuchullain
    spake:
'Welcome howe'er thou com'st, Ferdīa! Once
In Scatha's isle far otherwise thou camest
Morn after morn with tidings fresh of war
Plaything and pastime of our brother swords.
This day thou com'st invader of my land
Murthemné, bulwark broad of Uladh's realm;
Thou com'st to burn my cities, spoil my flocks—
A change there is, Ferdīa!' Stern of brow
The Firbolg answered; 'Friends we were: not
    peers:
The younger thou. 'Twas thine to yoke my
    steeds

THE COMBAT AT THE FORD. 169

Arm me for fight. A stripling hopes this day
With brandished spear to make a mountain flee!
Son of the Gael! long centuries since, thy race
Trampled my race:—their vengeance hour is
    near;
I bid thee to depart!' To him his friend;
'Ferdīa, in the old days on Scatha's Isle
Thou wert my tribe, my house, my stock, my
    race!
Questioned I then on battle-plain, or when
On frosty nights we couched beneath one rug,
Ancestral claims, traditions of the clan?—
A change there is, Ferdīa!'
                      Thus with words
Or mild, or stern in hope to save not slay,'
Those friends contended. Sternest was the man
Whose conscience most aggrieved him.
                        'To this Ford
Thou cam'st the first, old comrade! choice of arms
Is therefore thine by right.' Cuchullain spake:
Ferdīa chose the javelin. Arrow-swift,
While still the charioteers brought back the shaft,
The missiles flew. Keen-eyed as ocean bird
That, high in sunshine poised, glimpses his prey
Beneath the wave, and downward swooping slays
    him,
Each watched the other's movements, if an arm
Lifted too high, or buckler dropped too low

Left bare a rivet. Long that fight endured:
Three times exhausted sank their hands: three
    times
They sat on rocks for respite, each the other
Eyeing askance, not silent; 'Lo the man
Who shields an ox-like or a swine-like race
That strikes no blow itself!' or thus; 'Ah pledge
Of amity eterne in old time sworn!
Ferdīa, vow thy vow henceforth to maids!
The man-race nothing heeds thee!'
                                  Evening fell
And stayed perforce that combat. Slowly drew
The warriors near; and as they noted, each,
The other bleeding, friendship unextinct
In all its strength returned: round either's neck
That other wound his arms and kissed him thrice:
That night their coursers in the self-same field
Grazed, side by side: that night their charioteers
With rushes gathered from the self-same stream
Made smooth their masters' beds, then sat them-
    selves
By the same fire. Cuchullain sent the half
Of every healing herb that lulled his wounds
To staunch Ferdīa's; while to him in turn
Ferdīa sent whate'er of meats or drinks
Held strengthening power or cordial, to allay
Distempered nerve or nimble spirit infuse,
In equal portions shared.

                    The second morn
They met at sunrise :—' Thine the choice of
    arms ;'
The Firbolg spake; the Gael made answer;
    ' Spears ! '
Then leaped the champions on their battle-cars
And launched them into battle. Dire their shock
In fiery orbits wheeling now; anon
Wheel locked in wheel. Profounder wounds by
    far
That day than on the first the warriors gored,
Since closer was the fight. With laughing lip
Not less that eve Cuchullain sang the stave
That chides in war ' Fomorian obstinacy :'
Again at eve drew near they, slower now
For pain, and interwove fraternal arms :
Again their coursers in the self-same field
Grazed side by side, and from the self-same stream
Again their charioteers the rushes culled :
Again they shared alike both meats and drinks,
Again those herbs allaying o'er their wounds
With incantations laid.
                    Forlorn and sad
Peered the third morning o'er the vaporous woods
The wan grey river with its floating weed,
And bubble unirradiate. From the marge
Cuchullain sadly marked the advancing foe:—
' Alas, my brother ! beamless is thine eye ;

The radiance lives no longer on thy hair;
And slow thy step.' The doomed one answered calm,
'Cuchullain, slow of foot, but strong of hand
Fate drags his victim to the spot decreed:
The choice to-day is mine: I choose the sword.'
    So spake the Firbolg: and they closed in fight:
And straightway from his heart to arm and hand
Rushed up the strength of all that buried race
By him so loved! Once more it swelled his breast:
Re-clothed in majesty each massive limb,
And flashed in darksome light of hair and eye
Resplendent as of old. Surpassing deeds
They wrought, while circled meteor-like their swords,
Then fell like heaven's own bolt on shield or helm.
Long hours they strove till morning's purer gleam
Vanished in noon. Sharper that day their speech;
For, in the intenser present, years gone by
Hung but like pallid, thin, horizon clouds
O'er memory's loneliest limit. Evening sank
Upon the dripping groves and shuddering flood
With rainy wailings. Not as heretofore
Their parting. Haughtily their mail they tossed
Each to his followers. In the self-same field
That night their coursers grazed not; neither sat

Their charioteers beside the self-same fire :
Nor sent they, each to other, healing herbs.
    Ere morn the Firbolg drank the strength of
    dreams
Picturing his race's wrong ; and trumpet blasts
Swept o'er him blown from fields of ancient wars,
And thus he mused, half-wakened ; 'Not for
    Meave ;
Not for the popular suffrage ; not for her
That maid who fain had held me from the snare,
Fight I that fight whose end shall crown this day.
O race beloved, this day your vengeance dawns
Red in the East ! The mightiest of the Gaels
Goes down before me. What if both should die ?
So best ! Thus too the Firbolg is avenged ! '
Thus mused he. Stately from his couch he rose,
And armed himself, sedate. Upon his breast
He laid, in iron sheathed, a huge, flat stone,
For thus he said, ' Though many a feat of arms
Is mine, from Scatha learned, or else self-taught,
The Gae-Bulg is Cuchullain's ! ' On his head
He fixed his helm, and on his arm his shield
Sable as night, with fifty bosses bound,
All brass ; the midmost like a noontide sun.
    Cuchullain eyed him as he neared the Ford
And spake to Leagh ; 'This day, if thou should'st
    mark
This hand or slack or sluggish, hurl, as wont,

Sharp storm of arrowy railing from thy lips
That so the battle-anger from on high
May flame on me.' The choice of arms was his:
He chose 'the Ford-Feat.' On the Firbolg's brow
A shadow fell :—'All weapons there,' he mused,
'Have place alike: if on him falls the rage
He will not spare the Gae-bulg!'*
                                        Well they knew,
Both warriors, that the fortunes of that day
Must end the conflict; that for one, or both,
The sun that hour ascending shone his last:
Therefore all strength of onset till that hour
By each or loosed or hoarded, craft of fight
Reined in one moment but to spring the next
Forward in might more terrible, compared
With that last battle was a trivial thing;
Whilst every weapon, javelin, spear, or sword,
Lawful alike that day, scattered abroad
Huge flakes of dinted mail; from every wound
Bounded the life-blood of a heart athirst
For victory or for death. The vernal day
Panted with summer ardours, while aloft
Noontide, a fire-tressed Fury, waved her torch,
Kindling the lit grove and its youngling green
From the azure-blazing zenith. As the heat
So waxed the warriors' frenzy. Hours went by:

---

* The Gae-bulg was a terrible weapon of war, almost always fatal, but which hardly any warrior was able to use.

That day they sought not rest on rock or mound,
Held no discourse. Slowly the sun declined;
And as wayfarers oft when twilight falls
Advance with strength renewed, so they, refreshed,
Surpassed their deeds at morning. With a bound
Cuchullain, from the bank high springing, lit
Full on the broad boss of Ferdīa's shield,
His dagger-point down turned. With spasm of
    arm
Instant the Firbolg from its sable rim
Cast him astonished. Upward from the Ford
Again Cuchullain reached that shield: again
With spasm of knee Ferdīa flung him far,
While Leagh in scorn reviled him: 'As the flood
Shoots on the tempest's blast its puny foam;
The oak-tree casts its dead leaf on the wave;
The mill-wheel showers its spray; the shameless
    woman
Hurls on the mere that babe which was her shame,
So hurls Ferdīa forth that fairy-child
Whom men misdeemed for warrior!'
                         Then from heaven
Came down upon Cuchullain, like the night,
The madness-rage. The Foes confronted met:
Shivered their spears from point to haft: their
    swords
Flashed lightnings round them. Fate-compelled,
    their feet

Drew near, then reached, that stream which back-
    ward fled
Leaving its channel dry. While raged that fight
Cuchullain's stature rose, huge bulk, immense,
Ascending still : as high Ferdīa towered
Like Fomor old, or Nemed from the sea,
Those shields, their covering late from foot to
    helm,
Shrinking, so seemed it, till above them beamed
Shoulders and heads. So close that fight, their
    crests
That waved defiance, mingled in mid air ;
While all along the circles of their shields
And all adown their swords ran, mad with rage,
Viewless for speed the demons of dark moors
And war-sprites of the valleys, Bocanachs
And Banacahs, whose scream, so keen its edge,
Might shear the centuried forest as the scythe
Shears meadow grass. To these in dread response
Thundered far off from sea-caves billow-beat
And halls rock-vaulted 'neath the eternal hills,
That race Tuatha, giant once, long since
To pigmy changed, that forge from molten ores
For aye their clanging weapons, shield or spear,
On stony anvils, waiting the day decreed
Of vengeance on the Gael. That tumult scared
The horses of the host of Meave, that brake
From war-car or the tethering rope, and spread

Ruin around. Camp-followers first, then chiefs
Innumerable were dragged along, or lay
'Neath broken axle, dead. The end was nigh :
Cuchullain's shield splintered upon his arm
Served him no more ; and through his fenceless
    side
Ferdīa drave the sword. Then first the Gael
Hurled forth this taunt ; 'The Firbolg, bribed by
    Meave,
Has sold his ancient friend !' Ferdīa spake,
'No Firbolg he, that man in Scatha's isle,
Who won a maid, then left her !' Backward
    stepped
Cuchullain paces three : he reached the bank ;
He uttered low ; 'The Gae-Bulg !' Instant, Leagh
Within his hand had lodged it. Bending low,
Low as that stream,—the war-game's crowning
    feat,—
He launched it on Ferdīa's breast. The shield,
The iron plate beneath, the stone within it,
Like shallow ice-films 'neath a courser's hoof
Burst. All was o'er. To earth the warrior sank :
Dying, he spake : 'Not thine this deed, O friend—
'Twas Meave who winged that bolt into my heart !'
  Then ran Cuchullain to that great one dead,
And raised him in his arms, and laid him down
Beside the Ford, but on its northern bank,
Not in that realm by Ailill swayed and Meave :
  L

Long time he looked the dead man in the face;
Then by him fell in swoon. 'Cuchullain, rise!
The men of Erin be upon thee! Rise!'
Thus Leagh. He answered, waking; 'Let them
    come!
To me what profit if I live or die?
The man I loved is dead!'
                        But by the dead
Cuchullain stood; and thus he made lament:
'Ferdīa! On their head the curse descend
Who sent thee to thy death! We meet no more;
Never while sun, and moon, and earth endure.
  'Ferdīa! Far away in Scatha's isle
A great troth bound us and a vow life-long
Never to raise war-weapons each on each:—
'Twas Finobar that snared thee! She shall die.
  'Ferdia! dearer to my heart wert thou
Than all beside if all were joined in one:
Dear was thy clouded face, and darksome eye;
Thy deep, sad voice; thy words so wise and few;
Dear was thy silence: dear thy slow, grave ways,
Not boastful like the Gael's.'
                            Silent he stood
While Leagh in reverence from the dead man's
    breast
Loosened his mail. There shone the torque of
    Meave:
There where the queen had fixed it yet it lay.

Cuchullain clutched it. 'Ha! that torque I
   spurned!
Dark gem ill-lifted from the seas of Death!
Swart planet bickering from the heavens of Fate!
With what a baleful beam thou look'st on me!
'Twas thou, 'twas thou not I, that slew'st this
   man'—
He dashed it on the rock, and with his heel
Crushed it to fragments.
                  Then, as one from trance
Waking, once more he spake: 'O me—O me,
That I should see that face so great and pale!
To-day face-whitening death is on that face;
And in my hand my sword :—'tis crimson yet.
That day when he and I triumphed in fight
By Formait's lake o'er Scatha's pirate foes
The woman fetched a beaker forth of wine,
And made us drink it both; and made us vow
Friendship eterne. O friend, my hand this day
Tendered a bloody beaker to thy lip.'
   Again he sang; 'Queen Meave to Uladh's bound
Came down; and dark the deed that grew thereof;
Came down with all the hosting of her kings;
And dark the deed that grew thereof. We two
Abode with Scatha in her northern isle,
Her pupils twinned. The sea-girt warrioress
That honoured few men honoured us alike :
We ate together of the self-same dish :

We couched together 'neath the self-same shield :
Now living man I stand, and he lies dead !'
  He raised again his head : once more he sang :
'Each battle was a game, a jest, a sport
Till came, fore-doomed, Ferdīa to the Ford.
I loved the warrior though I pierced his heart.
Each battle was a game, a jest, a sport
Till stood, self-doomed, Ferdīa by the Ford.—
Huge lion of the forestry of war ;
Fair, central pillar of the House of Fame ;
But yesterday he towered above the world :
This day he lies along the earth, a shade.'

SCENES FROM 'ALEXANDER THE GREAT.'

ALEXANDER AT TROY,

ANOINTING THE PILLAR ON THE GRAVE OF ACHILLES.

(Act I. Scene IV.)

                Mighty Sire, Achilles !
Lift from the dimness of the dolorous realm
Thy face upon thy son ! In it—I see it—
Survives, though sad, the unvanquishable youth ;
In it alone. The phantom of a spear
Is all that now can weight that phantom hand

Which awed the Atridæ ; and as though chain-
  bound
Move the swift feet that once outsped thy Mother's
Bounding from wave to wave ; yet, not the less,
Monarch thou walkest. 'Mid the Strengthless
  Heads
That, reverent, round thee flock—like thee
  lamenting,
Despite the embalm'd purpureal airs, and gleam
Immeasurable of amaranthine meads,
Lamenting still the strenuous airs of earth
And blasts from battle-fields ; like thee detesting
That frustrate, stagnant, ineffectual bourne
Where substance melts to shadow—lift, great king,
Once more from out the gloom a face sun-bright,
Elysium's wonder, on thy son's, and hear him :
To thee this day he consecrates his greatness :
Whate'er malign and intercepting Death
Detracted from thy greatness he concedes thee ;
Remands thee from the gulf the deed unborn ;
Yields thee, ere won, his victory and his empire.
This is the anointing, this the sacrifice,
Wherewith he crowns thy tomb.

ALEXANDER AT JERUSALEM.

(Act II. Scene VII.)

The Jewish High Priest, Alexander.

High Priest. This is that scroll whereof I spake
   to thee :
That Vision which the exiled prophet saw
Sitting in Susa, by Choaspes' flood :
' In vision I beheld a Beast two-horned ;
Westward he pushed, and northward, and to south,
Nor any stood before him. After that,
Another mightier portent, swifter far
Rushed from the west, o'er face of all the earth
Which yet he touched not, flying upon wings ;
He smote against that Beast, and trod him down ;
Nor any might deliver. Then, a Voice
There reached me from betwixt the river banks :
" That Beast which thou beheldest is that king,
Lord of the Median and the Persian realms :
He that shall overcome him is the Greek." '
This is that vision which our prophet saw.
   Alex. That Voice your prophet heard was Voice
       of God—   [*After musing.*]
You will not wed my cause, and save your city ?
   High Priest. We may not, and we will not.
   Alex.   Yet you know
Mine is the empire ?

High Priest.   What is writ is writ.
Alex. What was that sacrifice you offered late ?
The like I have not seen.
High Priest.   The shadow 'twas
Of substance onward striding. Ask no more :
We are a prophet-people : ours the Hope :
We are God's people, and we stand apart :
The kings of the earth may speed us, or may rend ;
Know us they cannot.
Alex.   I too had a vision—
I yield you credence, Priest. I have repented
My first resolve and fling it from me far :
I tribute none demand, and in your city
Challenge no rule.
Your prophets spake in ancient days of me;
Spake they in earlier days of Persian Cyrus ?
  High Priest. By name, before his birth two hundred years :
Hear thou God's edict : 'Cyrus is my shepherd :
I hold his right hand, loosening at his feet
The hearts of Monarchs. I will cut in twain
The bars of iron and the brazen gates.'
  Alex. The Babylonian gates stood wide that night
When back Euphrates shrank.
  High Priest (*reading*).   ' Be dry, ye rivers !
In Babylon the desert beast shall hide ;
The dragon couch within her palaces ;

The bittern shriek above her shallow pools.'
Young man, hold thou no hand to Babylon
For God hath judged her, lest thou share her plagues.
   Alex. Hers was the first of Empires and the worst—   [*After a pause.*]
The day goes by; lead onward to the gates.
O'er all the earth my empire shall be just,
Godlike my rule.
   High Priest. Young man, beware! God's prophet
Awards thee Persia's crown, but not the world's:
He who wears that should be the Prince of Peace.
Thy portion lies in bounds. Limit and Term
Govern the world. Thou know'st the Voice was God's
That spake. Two ways there are—between them choose.
   Alex. I shall not fail to meditate these twain,
Then make election.
   High Priest.   Pardon, royal sir,
A little moment past your choice was made:
'Tis known above; and you one day will know it.
You trust not God: the man you trust will fail you.
   Alex. What man?
   High Priest.   Yourself.
   Alex.   At least I trust none other.

High Priest. My message is delivered. Sir, farewell!

[HIGH PRIEST *departs.* PTOLEMY *enters.*]

Alex. There sits unwonted wonder on your brow,
My Ptolemy!

Ptol. Sir, all men kneel to you,
You but to one, and him a man unknown!
When first that long and strange procession reached
    us
I saw an earnest inquest in your eye,
A pallor on your cheek.

Alex. You err, my friend:
I knelt, but not to one unseen till then.
Three years gone by, three months, and twenty
    days,
At noon I sat in Macedonian Dium,
Musing the fortunes of this Asian war:
Then but decreed. There fell on me a trance
Filled with strange fear. Never save in that trance
Have I known fear.

Ptol. What saw you in it, Sir?

Alex. Things as they were.

Ptol. No more?

Alex. Yea, things beside:
My captains grew ape-visaged, and chattering
    rushed
On errands all confused, while down the street,
In the wide Agora, on the temple's steps,

The concourse, shrunk to pigmies, screamed and
    strove;—
The tallest like a three years' child. Meanwhile,
There where benignant plains had spread but late
Heaven-high there hung in the east a mount, fire-
    crowned,
And ruin-flanked—a mount which seemed a world
Huger than man's. The pigmies and the apes
Saw it and laughed.

    Ptol.   'Twas strange!
    Alex.   It was not slumber:
Parmenio and Philotas at my right
You, Ptolemy, at my left, witnessed and sware
That from my session ta'en till, sunset nigh,
The priesthood issued from the fane of Zeus,
I had not ceased from audience and command
Though sterner than my wont. The trance was
    long,
And, as it deepened, darkness closed around.
Then from that darkness like a god this man
Drew near, methought, that mitre on his brow,
That gem-illumined breast-plate on his breast.
He spake,—'Fear nought; the God I serve shall
    lay
His hand upon thy head and lead thee on
Triumphant through the danger and the gloom.'
This world is full of wonders, Ptolemy,
Or else it were not world for man, since man

Is marvellous most. Divulge this thing to none,
Nor write it in thine annals of the war.

A PORTRAIT OF ALEXANDER.

(Act III. Scene I.)

Parmenio *and* Philotas.

Phi. You are a greater man, sir, than you know
And bear your honours meekly. Pray you pardon
My sometimes halting reverence.
Par. Here's a change !
I have warned you oft to bate your perilous pride
Saying, 'My son be less.' Your whim is now
To show all humbleness.
Phi. I should be humble
To one who for his master has a god :
Unseen I heard the king expound his schemes,
Hephestion mildly plausive.
Par. Schemes ! What schemes ?
Phi. Kneel, Hercules, and Dionysus tremble !
Tremble, thou Caucasus that hid'st thy head
In snows eterne ! Our great stage-king has sworn
To plant his buskin on thy wintry scalp !
Par. What seeks the boy ?
Phi. From eastern Caucasus
Two rivers rush, the Indus and the Oxus,
One south, one north. He'll tie them, tail to tail,

Like foxes caught, to test their strength and
    prowess;
Next, on those heights he seeks some herb to
    enrich
The Stagyrite's medicine shop: and, lastly, thence
He'll o'er-gaze Scythia, which with proximate place
Is honoured in the order of his conquests.

    Par. Renounce great Persia for a realm of bears!
I march with him no more!

    Phi.   You shall not need:
Besieging Tyre, he sent you to Damascus
To seal up sacred balms, and perfume-phials,
And inventory the wardrobe of Darius.
In Egypt you had no conspicuous place:
Now, for like cause, the Caspian Gates you pass
    not,
Ecbatana your charge. Upon his treasure
He bids you sit like an old hen, and hatch it
While he strides on to victory. Snows of age
With what auspicious calm ye crown old heads!
And hearts virile no more!

    Par.   The king's a madman :—
The worse for us! Free him from that conceit
That he's a god, the man of men were he:
Since Marathon we have seen none other like him.

    Phi. One-half his victories come but of his blind-
    ness,
And noting not the hindrance.

Par.   At Granicus—
But that was chance. At Issus he was greater:
I set small store on Egypt or on Tyre :
Next came Arbela. Half a million foes
Melted like snow. To him Epaminondas
Was as the wingless creature to the winged.
    Phi. I grant his greatness were his godship sane !
But note his brow ; 'tis Thought's least earthly
    temple :
Then mark beneath, that round, not human eye
Still glowing like a panther's ! In his body
No passion dwells, but all his mind is passion,
Wild intellectual appetite and instinct
That works without a law.
    Par.   But half you know him:
There is a zigzag lightning in his brain
That flies in random flashes yet not errs :
His victories seem but chances :—link those
    chances
And under them a science you shall find
Though unauthentic, contraband, illicit,
Yea, contumelious oft to laws of war.
Fortune, that as a mistress smiles on others,
Serves him as duty-bound : her blood is he,
Born in the purple of her royalties.

PARMENIO'S BANISHMENT.

(ACT III. SCENE III.)

Alex. Caitiff and coward !
The grey hair—well thou know'st it—saves that head
Which else this sword had from thy shoulders swept !
I am requited justly who, unjustly
In glorious offices above thy peers
Stayed thee so long, for those high tasks unmeet
Which by Hephestion or by Ptolemy
In silence were vicariously discharged.
I strip thee of all functions to the last :—
Take from him chain and sword ! [*After a pause.*
I stand rebuked ;
And, gazing on your countenances, lords,
Remember that the ruins of a man
Have in them ruin's claims.
The man who smote his king upon the face,
Who on his forehead nailed the name of liar,
Shall live, but not beside him, and not near,
Honours shall keep, but sway no battle field.
Back to Ecbatana ! Get thee hence, Parmenio !
And guard its citadel with Harpalus
A pardoned man like thee. My purpose stood
Thou thence shouldst join us with our Thracian aids :

It shall not be; for I distrust thy sword
Though one time sharp, distrust, detest thy
    counsel,
Yet trust thy faithfulness to guard my gold
And keep my Median capital in awe.
Depart: work waits. Thy son shall take no hurt
From his sire's fall. On earth we meet no more.
    Par. King—for that pride which maddens and
        will wreck you
Demands such lessening titles—I depart.
I too, like you, have mused, and changed my
        purpose :
That which it was and is let no man ask.
This is the ending of a life-long league—
I laid my strong sword by your cradle's side ;
I taught you how to walk, and how to run,
To ride, to swim ; and when you sought to fly
I bade you to beware.
Could all this thing be painted, patched, adjusted
Reduced to spleen of fancy, proven a dream,
This day from out the starry count of time
Be blotted, cancelled, buried, and trod out
I'd not so have it for my heart is changed.
My head, you say, through age hath lost its
        cunning ;
My heart hath insight still : I see your end :
I'll whisper it to Philip in the shades
For I shall see him soon.

You shall succeed, and your success be ruin:
A name you shall achieve: in after years
The byeword it shall live of madness crowned:
By night the dagger and the spear by day
From you shall glance: snow-wastes and burning
    sands
To you obsequious shall but choke the just;
Yet all your greatness shall be changed to bane.
Your virtues shall not walk in Virtue's ways
But glorify your vices, and the beam
Of your bright mind blacken that mind to mad-
    ness.
The empire you shall build in cloudy wreck
Shall melt around your deathbed premature
Which shall not be a warrior's: that first realm
Your father's work and mine, to dust shall fall,
The Royal house evanish as a wind,
Your mother, and your sisters, sons, and wife .
Struck down successive by a vassal hand
In bloody base and ignominious death.
Lords, give ye way! Some blood-drops in my
    brain
At times make dim mine eyes; but help I need
    not.
Who's this? Hephestion? Tell my son, Philotas,
That after-musings on this morn's discourse
Have somewhat changed my sentence. Home,
    they say,

Is best for age. I seek it. Eighty years
I've made my home on horseback. Sirs, farewell.

ALEXANDER'S AMBITION.

(Act III. Scene IX.)

ALEXANDER and HEPHESTION.

Alex. Resume we our dispute !
What if the race of gods began with men ?
If Nature, evermore through strife educing
Stronger from strong, throned on Olympus first
The heroic-proved of men as demi-gods,
And these through strife worked out the gods that rule ?
Concede me this as true and man's ambition
Kindred may claim with gods.
   Heph. Concede it ! never :
Greatness, be sure, came never from below :
That thought would drag from heaven itself its greatness :
Rather the gods themselves make manifest
One higher far than they.
Sir, there are whispers, trust me, from beneath—
These should be trampled and not parleyed with :
Esteem such thoughts among them.
   Alex. This, that's great
My thought suggests ; an infinite progression.
   Heph. Nay, but a finite mocking infinite,

And murdering what it mocks ;— the highest term
In such a series but repeats the first,
Exaggerating still inherent flaws,
And in a nakeder shape though vaster scale
Showing man's nature shamed.
 Alex.   The gods have passions,
Not minds alone : in this they are like to men.
 Heph. They act like men who have them :—that
  proves little :
Our ignorance doubtless misconceives their acts :
'Twas not Apollo's spite that sentenced Marsyas :
'Twas no earth-instinct on Endymion smiled:
The self-same acts, in gods, in men, in beasts,
Know difference large. Acts lawful in the man
Are crimes in boys.
 Alex.   A race of gods hath fallen :
Then Zeus in turn may fall. I find no thrones
Whereon the gods themselves may sit secure ;
I find to man's advance no term or limit ;
No certain truth amid contending rites ;
No base for Faith.
 Heph.   Then man must live by Hope
 Alex. And whence our hope?
 Heph. From all things good around us,
From all things fair—the brightness of the
  world,
The glory of its rivers and its seas,
The music in the wandering of its winds,

The magic in the spring-flowers fresh accost,
The gladdening sweetness and pure grace of
  woman,
The questioning eyes of childhood. With one
  voice
They preach one hope—that virtue shall be crowned
One day, and Truth be known.

ALEXANDER'S LAST ILLNESS.

(Act V. Scene VIII.)

Alexander and Ptolemy.

Alex. We're stayed in the midst.
Ptol. Sire, may the mighty gods——
Alex. I'm hindered of my own : my march is
  hindered !
That march was ordered for the third day hence :
This bends it to the fifth.
Ptol. Too quickly pass——
Alex. Thus much the malice of o'er-weening
  gods,
Or else their negligence, can fret our course !
I'm maimed, and tamed, and shamed : but mind
  can act
When the outward act is barred. Six audiences
I have given. The chief of my Thessalian horse
Had failed to impress his blacksmiths. Nehordates
Had sent no corn to Opis.

Ptol.   Sire, your eyes
Are blood—all blood. Where is it you feel the pain?
   Alex. I have wrestled oft with pain and flung it ever:
Save for that fire in brain, and heart, and hand,
I am well enough. My strength as yet is whole.
To work! You need the map. Despatch, this even,
Heraclides to the Caspian, there to build
A fleet for exploration: let him search
If thence a passage lead not to the Euxine:
That found, a six weeks' march were spared and more
Twixt Hellespont and Indus.
   Ptol.   One hour, my king,
But one, give rest to that—
   Alex.   Recall Nearchus:
Command that he forbear those Arab pirates:
Bid him through help of theirs—an army with him—
Circle all Afric, reach the Atlantic Pillars:
Thence eastward curving on the midland sea
He'll meet, near Carthage, or that coast Numidian,
Our westward-marching host. You're staring, sir!
   Ptol. All shall be done.
   Alex.   Ere sunset send to Egypt:

We need a road to coast her sea. Her sands
Are fire that blasts my eyes.
    Ptol.   The brain o'er-heated
Recalls Gedrosia's waste.
    Alex.   My brain's not touched :
I watch it : if there rise beyond its verge
A cloud, the slenderest, of bewildered thought
You'll learn it thus—I close my lips for ever.
    Ptol. Your thoughts are strong, my king, dis-
        tinct, and plain.
    Alex. A light of conflagration makes them
        plain :
'Tis sent as from a pyre.
    Ptol.   Immortal gods !
Grant to this sufferer the balm of sleep !
    Alex. Sleep ! Can you guard me 'gainst ill
        dreams in slumber ?
I'll tell you one. I died ; and lay in death
A century 'mid those dead Assyrian kings
In their old tomb by yonder stagnant lake.
Then came a trumpet-blast that might have waked
Methought a sleeping world. It woke not them.
I could not rise : I could not join the battle :
Yet I saw all.
    Ptol.   What saw you, sire ?
    Alex.   Twelve tents,
Each with my standard. On twelve hills they
        stood

Which either on their foreheads blazoned wore,
Or from my spirit's instinct took great names,
Cithæron, Hæmus, Taurus, Libanus,
Parapomisus, and huge Caucasus,
With other five, and Athos in the midst.
Then from my royal tents on those twelve hills
Mailed in mine arms, twelve Alexanders crowned
With all their armies rushed into a plain
Which quaked for fear, and dashed across twelve floods,
Euphrates, Issus, Tigris, Indus, Oxus,
And others with great names. They met—those Twelve—
And, meeting, swelled in stature to the skies,
And grappled breast to breast and fought and died,
Save four that, bleeding, each on other stared,
And leaned upon their swords. As thus they stood,
Slow from that western heaven which domes the accursed—
Rome's bandit brood—there moved a cloud night-black,
Which onward-gathering mastered all the East
And o'er it rained a rain of fire. The earth
Split, and the rivers twelve in darkness sank;
The twelve great mountains which had borne my standard

Rifted and splintered crumbled to the plain;
The bones of those twelve armies ceased from sight:
Then from the sun that died and dying moon
And stars death-sentenced fell great drops of blood
Large as their spheres till all the earth was blood;
And o'er that blood-sea rang a female cry,
'The Royal House is dead.'
   Ptol.   My king, my friend—
   Alex. Phylax is dust. You cannot bid him
      tend me!
   Ptol. Olympias, prescient, sent you, sire, from
     . Greece
But late its wisest leech. How oft you've said
'A mother's prayers are hard to be withstood!'
   Alex. I loved her in the old days: nor years,
      nor wars
Disturbed that image. But a greater love
In its great anguish tramples out all others.
Impostors are they all—those heart-affections:
They're dupes that make us dupes—
There's not on earth a confidence unflawed.
I think *he* kept from me at Tyre a secret
Touching that princess. I from him concealed
That warning strange at Hierosolyma
Whereof it may be my contempt more late
When, old Parmenio doomed, I marched to India
Bore me ill fruit. Betwixt that warning strange
And this my sickness was there aught in common?

Ptol. It may be, sire, there was.
Alex.   Ere yet that darkness
Hurled by injurious and malignant Fates
Against this unsubverted head, had found me—
The Fates that hustle heroes out of life;
The Fates that hustled gods into the abyss;
The unobsequious Fates that mock at all things—
In diligent musings at Ecbatana
I thus resolved;—to see once more that priest:
Then came that death—
And in the gloomy raptures of just wrath
That mood went by. I marched to Babylon:
Then came the end. Who sings?
   Ptol.   Poor Hebrew slaves;
They weed the palace court.

The Song.

Behold, He giveth His Belovèd sleep,
   And they shall waken in a land of rest:
Behold, He leadeth Israel like a sheep:
   His pasture is the mountain of the Blest.
Blessed are they whose hands are pure from guilt;
   Who bore the yoke from childhood, yet are free:
Jerusalem is as a city built
   Wherein the dwellers dwell in unity.

   Alex. That song's amiss.
   Ptol.   Sire, for your army's sake

Which like a wounded warrior moans in sleep,
Your Empire's sake, that, immature and weak
Is threatened in its cradle—
    Alex.   'Tis so : 'tis so :
It lacks completion ; and the years, the months,
The hours, like ravening wolves that hunt a stag
Come up upon my haunches. Six o' the clock
On the fifth morn ! At noon we cross Euphrates :
That hour you'll learn my plans;
I'll cast this sickness from me like the rags
Flung from some lazar house ! Whose step is that ?
    Ptol. Sire, there is none.
    Alex.   Let not Seleucus near me !
Those onsets of his blundering, blind devotion,
So unlike his that perished—
    Ptol.   Sire, none comes.
    Alex. Be strong ! What shall be must. Shake
        not : bend nearer !
I have a secret—one for thee alone :
'Twas not the mists from that morass disastrous,
Nor death of him that died, nor adverse gods,
Nor the Fates themselves ; 'twas something
        mightier yet
And secreter in the great night, that slew me.
                        [SELEUCUS *enters.*
Welcome, Seleucus !
    Sel.   Sire, I come unbidden
This Ptolemy—has Greece but one who loves you ?

Alex. Welcome, my brave Seleucus! In five days
We march, at earliest dawn. A month shall find us
Nighing old Egypt's coast. This scroll be yours:
It is a code for Alexandria's rule.
Therein I have made you lord. Till morn, farewell.
　　　　　　　　[SELEUCUS *departs reluctantly.*
I note you shaken, Ptolemy: learn thence
Philosophy's a crutch for strength to play with:
It mocks us when we're weak. On the fifth day—
Farewell. 　　　　[*As* PTOLEMY *is departing.*
　　　　Return. Your tablets—I would see them.
Write down—the duty this of Eumenes—
He cheats his tasks—write down my burial place.
Likeliest you guess it.
　Ptol.　　　　　　　Macedonian Pella?
Old ties are strong. You said when leaving Greece,
'Pella, not Athens, if I die.'
　Alex.　　　　　　　Not Pella.
　Ptol. This Babylon where he you loved lies dead?
　Alex. 'Mid sands Egyptian—by the Ammonian grove—
In my great Father's fane.

A SOLILOQUY.

(ACT V. SCENE IX.)

ARSINOE (*on a balcony*).

       Silent stars
That flash from yonder firmament serene
Ye have no portion in these pangs of earth ;
Ye mock not man with infirm sympathy :
I thank you for your clear, unpitying brightness
That freezes Time's deceits. The Lord of Light
Sternly in you hath writ his four great Names—
Truth, Justice, Wisdom, Order. Ye endure :
Our storms sweep o'er you but they shake you not :
Darkness, our foe, but brings your hour of triumph :
Your teaching is—to bear.
       The Lord of Light—
Is it a woman's weakness that would wish him
Another, tenderer name, the Lord of Love ?
A love that out of love created all things :
A love that, warring ever, willeth peace ;
A patient love, from ill educing good ;
A conquering love, triumphant over death ?—
Ah me ! No land there is that clasps this Faith !
To hold it were to feel from Heaven a hand
Laid on the aching breast of human kind,

Laid on our own, and softer than the kiss
Of some imagined babe. Come quickly Death;
Beyond thy gate is Truth.

DEATH OF ALEXANDER.

(Act V.   Scene X.)

PTOLEMY *and* SELEUCUS.

Ptol. The greatest spirit that ever trod this earth
Hath passed from earth. He swifter than the
    morn
O'er-rushed the globe. Expectant centuries
Condensed themselves into a few brief years
To work his will; and all the buried ages
Summed their old wealth, to enrich, for man's
    behoof,
With virtuous wisdom one Olympian mind
Which, grappling all things—needing not expe-
    rience—
Yet scorned no diligence, the weapon shaped,
Itself, that hewed its way, nor left to others
The pettiest of those cares that, small themselves,
Are rivets which make whole the mail of greatness.
The world hath had its conquerors : one alone
Conquered for weal of them who bowed beneath
    him
And in the vanquished found his firmest friends
And passionatest mourners.

The world hath had its kings : but one alone
To whom a kingdom meant a radiant fabric
No tyrant's dungeon-keep, no merchant's mart,
But all-intelligential, so combining
All interests, aspirations, efforts, aims,
That man's great mind, therein made one o'er earth,
Might show all knowledge in its boundless glass
As the sea shows the sun. Rough Macedon,
Boast; yet be just! Thou wert this Wonder's nurse :
A mightier was his mother. Earth, take back
Thy chief of sons ! Henceforth his tomb art thou.
  Sel. Lords, he has gone who made us what we are ;
And we remanded to our nothingness
Have that, not words, to offer him for praise.
There stand among us some that watched his boyhood ;
They have had their wish—he lived his life. The gods,
Feared they the next step of their earthly rival
Who pressed so near their thrones ? Your pardon lords !
He's dead who should this day have praised the dead.
Happiest in this, he died before his friend.
Lords, we have lived in festival till now

 And knew it not. The approaching woes, they best
Shall measure greatness gone. The men who 'scape
Building new fortunes on the wreck-strewn shore
Shall to their children speak in life's sad eve
Of him who made its morning. Let them tell
His deeds but half or no man will believe them :
It may be they will scarce themselves believe,
Deeming the past a dream. That hour, their tears
Down-streaming, unashamed, like tears in sleep
Will better their poor words : who hear shall cry,
Pale with strong faith, 'There lived an Alexander.'

CÆDMON THE COWHERD, THE FIRST ENGLISH POET.

CÆDMON, a cowherd, being at a feast, declares when the harp reaches him that he cannot sing. As he sleeps, a divine Voice commands him to sing. He obeys, and the gift of song is imparted to him. Hilda, Abbess of Whitby, enrols him among her monks ; and in later years he sings the revolt of the Fallen Angels, and many Christian mysteries, thus becoming the first English poet.

ALONE upon the pleasant bank of Esk
Cædmon the Cowherd stood. The sinking sun
Reddened the bay, and fired the river-bank,
And flamed upon the ruddy herds that strayed

Along the marge, clear-imaged. None was nigh :
For that cause spake the Cowherd, 'Praise to God !
He made the worlds ; and now, by Hilda's hand
Planteth a crown on Whitby's holy crest :
Daily her convent towers more high aspire :
Daily ascend her Vespers. Hark that strain !'
He stood and listened. Soon the flame-touched
    herds
Sent forth their lowings, and the cliffs replied,
And Cædmon thus resumed : ' The music note
Rings through their lowings dull, though heard by
    few !
Poor kine, ye do your best ! Ye know not God,
Yet man, his likeness, unto you is God,
And him ye worship with obedience sage,
A grateful, sober, much-enduring race
That o'er the vernal clover sigh for joy,
With winter snows contend not. Patient kine,
What thought is yours, deep-musing ? Haply this:
" God's help ! how narrow are our thoughts, and
    few !
Not so the thoughts of that slight human child
Who daily drives us with her blossomed rod
From lowland valleys to the pails long-ranged !"
Take comfort, kine ! God also made your race !
If praise from man surceased, from your broad
    chests
That God would perfect praise, and, when ye died,

Resound it from yon rocks that gird the bay;
God knoweth all things. Let that thought suffice!'

    Thus spake the ruler of the deep-mouthed kine:
They were not his; the man and they alike
A neighbour's wealth. He was contented thus:
Humble he was in station, meek of soul,
Unlettered, yet heart-wise. His face was pale;
Stately his frame, though slightly bent by age:
Slow were his eyes, and slow his speech, and slow
His musing step; and slow his hand to wrath;
A massive hand, but soft, that many a time
Had succoured man and woman, child and beast,
And yet could fiercely grasp the sword. At times
As mightily it clutched his ashen goad
When like an eagle on him swooped some thought:
Then stood he as in dream, his pallid front
Brightening like eastern sea-cliffs when a moon
Unrisen is near its rising.

                      Round the bay
Meantime, as twilight deepened, many a fire
Up-sprang and horns were heard. Around the steep
With bannered pomp and many a tossing plume
Advancing slow a cavalcade made way.
Oswy, Northumbria's King, the foremost rode,
Oswy triumphant o'er the Mercian host,
Invoking favour on his sceptre new;

With him an Anglian prince, student long time
In Bangor of the Irish, and a monk
Of Frankish race far wandering from the Marne :
They came to look on Hilda, hear her words
Of far-famed wisdom on the Interior Life ;
For Hilda thus discoursed : ' True life of man
Is life within : inward immeasurably
The being winds of all who walk the earth ;
But he whom sense hath blinded nothing knows
Of that wide greatness : like a boy is he,
A boy that clambers round some castle's wall
In search of nests, the outward wall of seven,
Yet nothing knows of those great courts within,
The hall where princes banquet, or the bower
Where royal maids discourse with lyre and lute,
Much less its central church and sacred shrine
Wherein God dwells alone.' Thus Hilda spake ;
And they that gazed upon her widening eyes
Low whispered, each to each, 'She speaks of things
Which she hath seen and known.'

On Whitby's height
The royal feast was holden : far below,
A noisier revel dinned the shore ; therein
The humbler guests made banquet. Many a tent
Gleamed on the yellow sands by ripples kissed ;
And many a savoury dish sent up its steam ;
The farmer from the field had brought his calf ;

Fishers that increase scaled which green-gulfed
    seas
From womb crystalline, teeming, yield to man;
And Jock, the woodsman, from his oaken glades
The tall stag, arrow-pierced. In gay attire
Now green, now crimson, matron sat and maid:
Each had her due: the elder, reverence most,
The lovelier that and love. Beside the board
The beggar lacked not place.

                        When hunger's rage
Sharpened by fresh sea-air was quelled, the jest
Succeeded, and the tale of foreign lands;
Yet, boast who might of distant chief renowned
His battle-axe, or fist that felled an ox,
The Anglian's answer was 'our Hilda' still:
'Is not her prayer trenchant as sworded hosts?
Her insight more than wisdom of the seers?
What birth like hers illustrious? Edwin's self,
Dëira's exile, next Northumbria's king,
Her kinsman was. Together bowed they not
When he of holy hand, missioned from Rome
Paulinus, o'er them poured the absolving wave
And joined to Christ? Kingliest was she, that
    maid
Who spurned earth-crowns!' More late the miller
    rose—
He ruled the feast, the miller old, yet blithe—

And cried, 'A song!' So song succeeded song,
For each man knew that time to chant his stave
But no man yet sang nobly. Last the harp
Made way to Cædmon lowest at the board :
He pushed it back, answering, 'I cannot sing :'
The rest around him flocked with clamour, 'Sing!
And one among them, voluble and small,
Shot out a splenetic speech : 'This lord of kine,
Our herdsman, grows to ox! Behold, his eyes
Move slow, like eyes of oxen!'
        Slowly rose
Cædmon, and spake : 'I note full oft young men
Quick-eyed, but small-eyed, darting glances round
Now here, now there, like glance of some poor bird
That lights on all things and can rest on none :
As ready are they with their tongues as eyes ;
But all their songs are chirpings backward blown
On winds that sing God's song by them unheard :
My oxen wait my service : I depart.'
Then strode he to his cow-house in the mead
Displeased though meek, and muttered, 'Slow of
  eye!
My kine are slow : if rapid I, my hand
Might tend them worse.' Hearing his step, the
  kine
Turned round their hornèd fronts ; and angry
  thoughts
Went from him as a vapour. Straw he brought,

And strewed their beds ; and they contented well
Laid down ere long their great bulks, breathing
    deep
Amid the glimmering moonlight. He, with head
Propped on a favourite heifer's snowy flank,
Rested, his deer-skin o'er him drawn. Hard days
Bring slumber soon. His latest thought was this :
'Though witless things we are, my kine and I,
Yet God it was who made us.'

                        As he slept,
Beside him stood a Man Divine, and spake :
'Cædmon, arise, and sing.' Cædmon replied
'My Lord, I cannot sing, and for that cause
Forth from the revel came I. Once, in youth
I willed to sing the bright face of a maid
And failed, and once a gold-faced harvest-field
And failed, and once the flame-eyed face of war
And failed again.' To him the Man Divine,
'Those themes were earthly. Sing !' And Cæd-
    mon said,
'What shall I sing, my Lord ?' Then answer
    came,
'Cædmon, stand up, and sing thy song of God.'

  At once obedient, Cædmon rose, and sang ;
And help was with him from great thoughts of old
Yearly within his silent nature stored,
That swelled, collecting like a flood which bursts

In spring its icy bar. The Lord of all
He sang; that God beneath whose Hand eterne,
Then when He willed forth-stretched athwart the
    abyss,
Creation like a fiery chariot ran,
Forth-borne on wheels of ever-living stars :
Him first he sang. The builder here below
From fair foundations rears at last the roof ;
But Song, a child of heaven, begins with heaven
The archetype divine, and end of all ;
More late descends to earth. He sang that hymn,
' Let there be light, and there was light ; ' and lo !
On the void deep came down the seal of God
And stamped immortal form. Clear laughed the
    skies ;
From circumambient deeps the strong earth brake,
Both continent and isle ; while downward rolled
The sea-surge summoned to his home remote.
Then came a second vision to the man
There standing 'mid his oxen. Darkness sweet,
He sang, of pleasant frondage clothed the vales,
And purple glooms ambrosial cast from hills
Now by the sun deserted, which the moon,
A glory new-created in her place,
Silvered with virgin beam, while sang the bird
Her first of love-songs on the branch first-
    flower'd—
Not yet the lion stalked. And Cædmon sang

O'er-awed, the Father of all humankind
Standing in garden planted by God's hand,
And girt by murmurs of the rivers four,
Between the trees of Knowledge and of Life,
With eastward face. In worship mute of God,
Eden's Contemplative he stood that hour,
Not her Ascetic, since, where sin is none,
No need for spirit severe.
      And Cædmon sang
God's Daughter, Adam's Sister, Child, and Bride,
Our Mother Eve. Lit by the matin star
That nearer drew to earth and brighter flashed
To meet her gaze, that snowy Innocence
Stood up with queenly port: she turned; she saw
Earth's King, mankind's great Father: taught by
  God,
Immaculate, unastonished, undismayed,
In love and reverence to her Lord she drew,
And, kneeling, kissed his hand : and Adam laid
That hand, made holier, on that kneeler's head,
And spake; 'For this shall man his parents leave,
And to his wife cleave fast.'
      When Cædmon ceased,
Thus spake the Man Divine : 'At break of day
Seek out some prudent man and say that God
Hath loosed thy tongue; nor hide henceforth thy
  gift.'
Then Cædmon turned, and slept among his kine

Dreamless. Ere dawn he stood upon the shore
In doubt : but when at last o'er eastern seas
The sun, long wished for, like a god upsprang
Once more he found God's song upon his mouth
Murmuring high joy ; and sought an ancient
    friend
And told him all the vision. At the word
He to the Abbess with the tidings sped
And she made answer, 'Bring me Cædmon here.'

Then clomb the pair that sea-beat mount of God
Fanned by sea-gale, nor trod, as others used,
The curving way, but faced the abrupt ascent
And halted not, so worked in both her will,
Till now between the unfinished towers they stood
Panting and spent. The portals open stood :
Cædmon passed in alone. Nor ivory decked
Nor gold, the walls. That convent was a keep
Strong 'gainst invading storm or demon hosts
And naked as the rock whereon it stood,
Yet, as a church, august. Dark, high-arched
    roofs
Slowly let go the distant hymn. Each cell
Cinctured its statued saint, the peace of God
On every stony face. Like caverned grot
Far off the western window frowned : beyond,
Close by, there shook an autumn-blazoned tree :
No need for gems beside of storied glass.

He entered last that hall where Hilda sat
Begirt with a great company, the chiefs
Far ranged from end to end. Three stalls cross-crowned
Stood side by side, the midmost hers. The years
Had laid upon her brows a hand serene;
There left a strenuous blessing. Levelled eyes
Sable, and keen, with meditative might
Conjoined the instinct and the claim to rule:
Firm were her lips and rigid. At her right
Sat Finan, Aidan's successor, with head
Snow-white, and beard that rolled adown a breast
Never by mortal passion heaved in storm,
A cloister of majestic thoughts that walked
Humbly with God. High in the left-hand stall
Oswy was throned, a man in prime, with brow
Less youthful than his years. Exile long past
Or deepening thought of one disastrous deed
Had left a shadow in his eyes. The strength
Of passion held in check looked lordly forth
From head and hand : tawny his beard ; his hair
Thick-curled and dense. Alert the monarch sat
Half turned, like one on horseback set that hears,
And he alone, the advancing trump of war.
Down the long gallery strangers thronged in mass
Dane or Norwegian, huge of arm through weight
Of billows oar-subdued, with stormy looks

Wild as their waves and crags ; Southerns keen-
    browed ;
Pure Saxon youths fair-fronted, with mild eyes—
These less than others strove for foremost place—
And Pilgrim travel-worn. Behind the rest,
And higher-ranged in marble-arched arcade,
Sat Hilda's sisterhood. Clustering they shone
White-veiled and pale of face and still and meek,
An inly-bending curve, like some young moon
Whose crescent glitters o'er a dusky strait.
In front were monks dark-stoled ; for Hilda ruled,
Though feminine, two houses, one of men :
Upon two chasm-divided rocks they stood,
To various service vowed though single Faith ;
Nor ever, save at rarest festival,
Their holy inmates met.
                    'Is this the man
Favoured, though late, with gift of song?' thus
    spake
Hilda with gracious smile. Severer then
She added : 'Son, the commonest gifts of God
He counts His best, and oft temptation blends
With ampler boon. Yet sing! That God who
    lifts
The violet from the grass could draw not less
Song from the stone hard by. That strain thou
    sang'st
Rehearse once more.'

Then Cædmon from his knees
Arose and stood. With princely instinct first
The strong man to the Abbess bowed, and next
To that great twain, the bishop and the king,
Last to that stately concourse each side ranged
Down the long hall; dubious he answered thus:
'Great Mother, if that God who sent the Song
Vouchsafe me to recall it, I will sing;
But I misdoubt it lost.' Slowly his face
Down-drooped, and all his body forward bent
While brooding memory, step by step, retraced
Its backward way. Vainly long time it sought
The starting-point. Then Cædmon's large, soft
    hands
Opening and closing worked; for wont were they
In musings when he stood, to clasp his goad
And plant its point far from him, thereupon
Propping his stalwart weight. Customed support
Now finding not, unwittingly those hands
Reached forth, and on Saint Finan's crosier staff
Settling, withdrew it from the old bishop's grasp;
And Cædmon leant thereon, while passed a smile
From chief to chief to see earth's meekest man
The spiritual sceptre claim of Lindisfarne.
They smiled: he triumphed: soon the Cowherd
    found
That first fair corner-stone of all his Song;
Thence rose the fabric heavenward. Lifting hands,

Once more his lordly music he rehearsed,
The void abyss at God's command forth-flinging
Creation like a Thought; where night had reigned,
The universe of God.
                    The singing stars
Which with the Angels sang when earth was made
Sang in his Song. From highest shrill of lark
To ocean's moaning under cliffs low-browed
And roar of pine-woods on the storm-swept hills,
No tone was wanting; while to them that heard
Strange images looked forth of worlds new-born,
Fair, phantom mountains, and with forests plumed
Heaven-topping headlands for the first time glassed
In waters ever calm. O'er sapphire seas
Green islands laughed. Fairer, the wide earth's flower,
Eden, on airs unshaken yet by sighs
From bosom still inviolate forth breathed
Immortal sweets that sense to spirit turned.
In part those noble listeners *made* that song!
Their flashing eyes, their hands, their heaving breasts,
Tumult self-stilled, and mute, expectant trance,
'Twas these that gave their bard his two-fold might—
That might denied to poets later born
Who, singing to soft brains and hearts ice-hard,
Applauded or contemned, alike roll round

A vainly-seeking eye, and, famished, drop
A hand clay-cold upon the unechoing shell,
Missing their inspiration's human half.

 Thus Cædmon sang, and ceased. Silent awhile
The concourse stood, for all had risen as though
Waiting from heaven its echo. Each on each
Gazed hard and caught his hands. Fiercely ere long
Their gratulating shout aloft had leaped
But Hilda laid her finger on her lip,
Or provident lest praise might stain the pure,
Or deeming song a gift too high for praise.
She spake: 'Through help of God thy Song is sound:
Now hear His Holy Word, and shape therefrom
A second hymn, and worthier than the first.'

 She spake, and Finan standing bent his head
Above the sacred tome in reverence stayed
Upon his kneeling deacon's hands and brow,
And sweetly sang five verses, thus beginning,
'*Cum esset desponsata*,' and was still;
And next rehearsed them in the Anglian tongue:
Then Cædmon took God's Word into his heart,
And ruminating stood, as when the kine,
Their flowery pasture ended, ruminate;
And was a man in thought. At last the light

Shone from his dubious countenance, and he
    spake :
'Great Mother, lo! I saw a second Song!
T'wards me it sailed ; but with averted face,
And borne on shifting winds. A man am I
Sluggish and slow, that needs must muse and
    brood;
Therefore those verses till the sun goes down
Will I revolve. If Song from God be mine
Expect me here at morn.'

                      The morrow morn
In that high presence Cædmon stood and sang
A second Song, and worthier than his first ;
And Hilda said, 'From God it came, not man ;
Thou therefore live a monk among my monks,
And sing to God.' Doubtful he stood—'From
    youth
My place hath been with kine; their ways I know,
And how to cure their griefs.' Smiling she spake,
'Our convent hath its meads, and kine ; with these
Consort each morn : at noon to us return.'
Then Cædmon knelt, and bowed, and said, 'So
    be it :'
And aged Finan, and Northumbria's king
Oswy, approved ; and all that host had joy.

    Thus in that convent Cædmon lived, a monk,
Humblest of all the monks, save him that knelt

In cell close by, who once had been a prince.
Seven times a day he sang God's praises, first
When earliest dawn drew back night's sable veil
With trembling hand, revisiting the earth
Like some pale maid that through the curtain peers
Round her sick mother's bed misdoubting half
If sleep lie there, or death; latest when eve
Through nave and chancel stole from arch to arch,
And laid upon the snowy altar-step
At last a brow of gold. In later years,
By ancient yearnings driven, through wood and
    vale
He tracked Dëirean or Bernician glades
To holy Ripon, or late-sceptred York
Not yet great Wilfrid's seat, or Beverley:
The children gathered round him, crying 'Sing!'
They gave him inspiration with their eyes,
And with his conquering music he returned it.
Oftener he roamed that strenuous eastern coast
To Jarrow and to Wearmouth, sacred sites
The well-beloved of Bede, or northward passed
To Bamborough, Oswald's keep. At Coldingham
His feet had rest; there where St. Ebba's Cape
That ends the lonely range of Lammermoor
Sustained for centuries o'er the wild sea-surge
In region of dim mist and flying bird,
Fronting the Forth, those convent piles far-kenned,
The worn-out sailor's hope.

Fair English shores,
Despite those blinding storms of north and east,
Despite rough ages blind with stormier strife,
Or frozen by doubt, or sad with worldly care,
A fragrance as of Carmel haunts you still
Bequeathed by feet of that forgotten Saint
Who trod you once sowing the seed divine!
Fierce tribes that kenned him distant round him
    flocked;
On sobbing sands the fisher left his net,
His lamb the shepherd on the hills of March,
Suing for song. With wrinkled face all smiles,
Like that blind Scian circling Grecian coasts,
If God the Song accorded, Cædmon sang;
If God denied it, after musings deep
He answered, 'I am of the kine and dumb;'—
The man revered his art, and fraudful song
Esteemed as fraudful coin.
                        Better than tale
They loved their minstrel's harp. The songs he
    sang
Were songs to brighten gentle hearts; to fire
Strong hearts with holier courage; hope to breathe
Through spirits despondent, o'er the childless floor
Or widowed bed flashing from highest heaven
A beam half faith, half vision. Many a tear
His own, and tears of those that listened, fell
Oft as he sang that hand lovely as light

Forth stretched, and gathering from forbidden
    boughs
That fruit fatal to man. He sang the Flood
Sin's doom that quelled the impure, yet raised to
    height
Else inaccessible, the just. He sang
That patriarch facing at divine command
The illimitable waste—then, harder proof,
Lifting his knife o'er him the seed foretold:
He sang of Israel loosed, the ten black seals
Down pressed on Egypt's testament of woe,
Covenant of pride with penance; sang the face
Of Moses glittering still from Sinai's rocks,
The Tables twain and Mandements of God.
On Christmas nights he sang that jubilant star
Which led the Magians to the Bethlehem crib
By Joseph watched and Mary. Pale, in Lent,
Tremulous and pale, he told of Calvary,
Nor added word, but, as in trance, rehearsed
That Passion fourfold of the Evangelists,
Which, terrible and swift—not like a tale—
With speed of things which must be done not said
A river of bale from guilty age to age
Along the astonied shores of common life
Annual makes way, the history of the world,
Not of one day, one People. To its fount
Time's stream he tracked, that primal mystery sang
Which, chanted later by a thousand years,

Music celestial though with note that jarred,
Some wandering orb troubling its starry chime,
Amazed the nations, 'There was war in heaven :
Michael and they, his angels, warfare waged
With Satan and his angels.' Brief that war
That ruin total. Brief was Cædmon's song :
Therein the Eternal Face was undivulged :
Therein the Apostate's form no grandeur wore :
The grandeur was elsewhere.

O holy House of Whitby ! on thy steep
Rejoice, howe'er the tempest, night or day,
Afflict thee, or the centuries slow to earth
Drag down thine airy arches' long suspense ;
Rejoice, for Cædmon in thy cloisters knelt,
And singing paced beside thy sounding sea !
Long years he lived ; and with the whitening hair
More youthful grew in spirit, and more meek ;
Yea, those who saw him said he sang within
Then when the golden mouth but seldom breathed
Sonorous strain, and when—that fulgent eye
No longer bright—still on his forehead shone
Not flame but purer light, that after-glow
Which, when the sunset woods no longer burn,
Maintains high place on Alpine throne remote
Or utmost beak of promontoried cloud
And heavenward dies in smiles. Esteem of men
Daily he less esteemed, through single heart
More knit with God. To please a sickly child

He sang his latest song, and, ending, said,
'Song is but body, though 'tis body winged :
The soul of song is love : the body dead,
The soul should thrive the more.' That Patmian
    Sage
Whose head had lain upon the Saviour's breast,
Who in high vision saw the First and Last,
Who heard the harpings of the Elders crowned,
Who o'er the ruins of the Imperial House
And ashes of the twelve great Cæsars dead
Witnessed the endless triumph of the Just,
That Sage, those glories ended, weak through age,
But seldom spake and gave but one command,
The great '*Mandatum Novum*' of his Lord,
'My children, love each other !' Like to his
Was Cædmon's age. Weakness with happy stealth
Increased upon him : he was cheerful still :
He still could pace, though slowly, in the sun,
Still gladsomely converse with friends who wept,
Still lay a broad hand on his well-loved kine.

    The legend of the last of Cædmon's days :—
That hospital wherein the old monks died
Stood but a stone's throw from the monastery :
'Make there my couch to-night,' he said, and
    smiled :
They marvelled, yet obeyed. There, hour by hour,
The man, low-seated on his pallet-bed,

In silence watched the courses of the stars,
Or casual spake at times of common things,
And three times played with childhood's days, and twice
His father named. At last, like one that long
Compassed with good, is smit by sudden thought
Of greater good, thus spake he : 'Have ye, sons,
Here in this house the Blessed Sacrament ?'
They answered, wrathful, 'Father, thou art strong;
Shake not thy children !   Thou hast many days !'
' Yet bring me here the Blessed Sacrament,'
Once more he said. The brethren issued forth
Save four that silent sat waiting the close.
Ere long in grave procession they returned,
Two deacons first, gold-vested ; after these
That priest who bare the Blessed Sacrament
And acolytes behind him, lifting lights.
Then from his pallet Cædmon slowly rose
And worshipped Christ, his God, and reaching forth
His right hand, cradled in his left, behold!
Therein was laid God's Mystery. He spake :
'Stand ye in flawless charity of God
T'ward me, my sons ; or lives there in your hearts
Memory the least of wrong ?' The monks replied :
'Father, within us lives nor wrong nor wrath

But love, and love alone.' And he: 'Not less
Am I in charity with you, my sons,
And all my sins of pride, and other sins,
Humbly I mourn.' Then, bending the old head
O'er the old hand, Cædmon received his Lord
To be his soul's viaticum, in might
Leading from life that seems to life that is;
And long, unpropped by any, kneeling hung
And made thanksgiving prayer. Thanksgiving made,
He sat upon his bed and spake: 'How long
Ere yet the monks begin their matin psalms?'
'That hour is nigh,' they answered; he replied,
'Then let us wait that hour,' and laid him down
With those kine-tending and harp-mastering hands
Crossed on his breast, and slept.
      Meanwhile the monks,
The lights removed in reverence of his sleep,
Sat mute nor stirred such time as in the Mass
Between *'Orate Fratres'* glides away,
And *'Hoc est Corpus Meum.'* Northward far
The great deep, seldom heard so distant, roared
Round those wild rocks half way to Bamborough Head;
For now the mightiest spring-tide of the year
Following the magic of a maiden moon,
Approached its height. Nearer, that sea which sobbed

In many a cave by Whitby's winding coast
Or died in peace on many a sandy bar
From river-mouth to river-mouth outspread,
They heard, and mused upon eternity
That circles human life. Gradual arose
A softer strain and sweeter, making way
O'er that sea-murmur hoarse; and they were ware
That in the black far-shadowing church whose bulk
Up-towered between them and the moon, the monks
Their matins had begun. A little sigh
That moment reached them from that central gloom
Guarding the sleeper's bed; a second sigh
Succeeded: neither seemed the sigh of pain;
And some one said, 'He wakens.' Large and bright
Over the church-roof sudden rushed the moon
And smote the cross above that sleeper's couch,
And smote that sleeper's face. The smile thereon
Was calmer than the smile of life. Thus died
Cædmon, the earliest bard of English song.

BEDE'S LAST MAY.

Bede issues forth from Jarrow, and visiting certain villagers in a wood, expounds to them the Beatitudes of Our Lord. Wherever he goes he seeks records of past times, and promises in return that he will bequeath to his fellow-countrymen translations from divers Sacred Scriptures, and likewise a history of God's Church in their land. Having returned to his monastery, he dies a happy death on the Feast of the Ascension, while finishing his translation of St. John's Gospel.

WITH one lay-brother only, blessed Bede,
In after times 'The Venerable' named,
Passed from his convent, Jarrow. Where the
    Tyne
Blends with the sea, all beautiful it stood
Bathed in the sunrise. At the mouth of Wear
A second convent, Wearmouth, rose. That hour
The self-same matin splendour gilt them both,
And in high speech of mingling lights, not words,
Both sisters praised their God.
                    'Apart, yet joined'—
So mused the old man gazing on the twain:
Then onward paced with head above his book
Murmuring his office. Algar walked behind,
A youth of twenty years, with tonsured head
And face though young forlorn. An hour had
    passed;
They reached a craggy height, and looking back
Beheld once more beyond the forest roof

Those two fair convents glittering—at their feet
Those two clear rivers winding! Bound by rule
Again the monk addressed him to his book;
Lection and psalm recited thus he spake:

    'Why placed our holy Founder thus so near
His convents! Why, albeit a single rule,
At last a single hand, had sway o'er both,
Placed them at distance? Hard it were to guess:
I know but this, that severance here on earth
Is strangely linked with union of the heart,
Union with severance. Thou hast lost, young
    friend,
But lately lost thy boyhood's dearest mate,
Thine earliest friend, a brother of thy heart,
True Christian soul though dwelling in the world;
Fear not such severance can extinguish love
Here, or hereafter! He whom most I loved
Was severed from me by the tract of years:
A child of nine years old was I when first
Jarrow received me: pestilence ere long
Swept from that house her monks, save one alone,
Ceolfrid, then its abbot. Man and child,
We two the lonely cloisters paced; we two
Together chaunted in the desolate church:
I could not guess his thoughts; to him my ways
Were doubtless as the ways of some sick bird
Watched by a child. Not less I loved him well:

Me too he somewhat loved. Beneath one roof
We dwelt—and yet how severed ! Save in God,
What know men, one of other ? Here on earth
Perhaps 'tis wiser to be kind to all
In large goodwill of helpful love, yet free,
Than link to one our heart—
Poor youth! that love which walks in narrow
 ways
Is tragic love, be sure.'
                          With gentle face
The novice spake his gratitude. Once more,
His hand upon the shoulder of the youth,
For now they mounted slow a bosky dell,
The old man spake—yet not to him—in voice
Scarce louder than the murmuring pines close
 by;
For, by his being's law he seemed, like them,
At times when pensive memories in him stirred,
Vocal not less than visible : 'How great
Was he, our Founder ! In that ample brow
What brooding weight of genius ! In his eye
How strangely was the pathos edged with light !
How oft, his churches roaming, flashed its beam
From pillar on to pillar, resting long
On carven imagery of flower or fruit,
Or deep-dyed window whence the heavenly choirs
Gave joy to men below ! With what a zeal
He drew the cunningest craftsmen from all climes

To express his thoughts in form ; while yet his
    hand,
Like meanest hand among us, patient toiled
In garden and in bakehouse, threshed the corn,
Or drave the calves to milk-pail ! Earthly rule
Had proved to him a weight intolerable ;
In Spiritual Beauty, there and there alone,
Our Bennet Biscop found his native haunt,
The lucent planet of his soul's repose:
And yet—O wondrous might of human love—
One was there, one, to whom his heart was
    knit,
Siegfried, in all unlike him save in worth.
His was plain purpose, rectitude unwarped,
Industry, foresight. On his friend's behalf
He ruled long years those beauteous convents
    twain,
Yet knew not they were beauteous ! An abyss
Severed in spirit those in heart so near:
More late exterior severance came: three years
In cells remote they dwelt by sickness chained:
But once they met—to die. I see them still:
The monks had laid them on a single bed ;
Weeping, they turned them later each to each;
I saw the snowy tresses softly mix ;
I saw the faded lips draw near and meet ;
Thus gently interwreathed I saw them die—
Strange strength of human love ! '

                              Still walked they on:
As high the sun ascended woodlands green
Shivered all golden; and the old man's heart
Brightened like them.   His ever active mind
Inquisitive took note of all it saw;
And as some youth enamoured lifts a tress
Of her he loves and wonders, so the monk,
Well loving Nature loved her in detail,
Now pleased with nestling bird, anon with flower,
Now noting how the beech from dewy sheath
Pushed forth its silken leaflets fringed with down,
Exulting next because from sprays of lime
The little fledgeling leaves, like creatures winged,
Brake from their ruddy shells.   Jesting, he cried:
'Algar! but hear those birds!   Men say they sing
To fire their young, shell-bound, with gladsome
        news
And bid them seek the sun!'   Sadly the youth
With downward front replied: 'My friend is
        dead;
For me to gladden were to break a troth.'
Upon the brow of Bede a shadow fell;
Silent he paced, then stopped: 'Forgive me,
        Algar!
Old men grow hard.   Yet boys and girls salute
The May: like them the old must have their
        maying;
This is perchance my last.'

                        As thus he spake
They reached the summit of a grassy hill ;
Beneath there wound a stream, upon its marge
A hamlet nestling lonely in the woods :
Its inmates saw the Saint and t'wards him sped
Eager as birds that, when the grain is flung
In fountained cloister-court of Eastern church,
From all sides flock with sudden rush of wings,
Darkening the pavement. Youths and maids came first ;
Their elders followed : men his garments kissed,
Women his hands. The venerable man
Stretched forth his arms as though to clasp them all :
Above them next he signed his Master's cross ;
Then, while the tears ran down his aged face,
Brake forth in grateful joy : 'To God the praise !
When, forty years ago, I roamed this vale
A haunt it was of rapine and of wars ;
Now see I pleasant pastures, peaceful homes,
And faces peacefuller yet. That God Who walked
With His disciples 'mid the sabbath fields
While they the wheat-ears bruised, His sabbath keeps
Within your hearts this day ! His harvest ye !
Once more a-hungered are His holy priests ;
They hunger for your souls ; with reverent palms
Daily the chaff they separate from the grain ;

Daily His Church within her heart receives you,
Yea, with her heavenly substance makes you
    one;
Ye grow to be her eyes that see His truth;
Her ears that hear His voice; her hands that
    pluck
His tree of life; her feet that walk His ways.
Honouring God's priests ye err not, O my friends;
Yea, thus ye honour God. In Him rejoice!'
    So spake he, and his gladness kindled theirs;
With it their courage. One her infant brought
And sued for him a blessing. One, bereaved,
Cried out: 'Your promised peace has come at
    last;
No more I wish him back to earth!' Again
Old foes shook hands; while now, their fears
    forgotten,
Children that lately nestled at his feet
Clomb to his knees. Then called from out that
    crowd
A blind man; 'Read once more that Book of
    God!
For, after you had left us, many a month
I, who can neither see the sun nor moon,
Saw oft the God-Man walking farms and fields
Of that fair Eastern land!' He spake, and lo!
All those around that heard him clamoured,
    'Read!'

Then Bede, the Sacred Scriptures opening, lit
Upon the 'Sermon on the Mount,' and read:
'The Saviour lifted up His holy eyes
On His disciples, saying, Blessed they;'
Expounding next the sense. 'Why fixed the Lord
His eyes on them that listened? Friends, His
    eyes
Go down through all things searching out the
    heart;
He sees if heart be sound to hold His word
And bring forth fruit in season, or as rock
Naked to bird that plucks the random seed.
Friends, with the heart alone we understand;
Who doth His will shall of the doctrine know
If His it be indeed. When Jesus speaks
Fix first your eyes upon His eyes divine,
There reading what He sees within your heart:
If sin He sees, repent!'
                              With hands upheld
A woman raised her voice, and cried aloud,
'Could we but look into the eyes of Christ
Nought should we see but love!' And Bede
    replied:
'From babe and suckling God shall perfect praise!
Yea, from His eyes looks forth the Eternal Love,
Though oft, through sin of ours, in sadness veiled;
But when he rests them on disciples true
Not on the stranger, love is love alone!

O great, true hearts that love so well your Lord !
That heard so trustingly His Tidings Good,
So long by trial proved have kept His Faith,
To you He cometh—cometh with reward
In heaven, and here on earth.'
                          With brightening face
As one who flingeth largess far abroad,
Once more he raised the sacred tome, and read,
Read loud the Eight Beatitudes of Christ ;
Once more the venerable man made pause,
Giving his Master's Blessings time to sink
Through hearts of those who heard. Anon with
    speech
Though fervent, grave, he showed the glory and
    grace
Of those majestic Virtues crowned by Christ
While virtues praised by worldlings passed un-
    named ;
How wondrously consentient each with each
Like flowers well sorted or like notes well joined :
Then changed the man to deeper theme ; he
    showed
How these high Virtues ere to man consigned
Were warmed and moulded in the God-Man's
    heart ;
Thence born, and in its sacred blood baptised.
'What are these Virtues but the Life of Christ ?
The poor in spirit : must not they be lowly

Whose God is One that stooped to wear our
    flesh ?
The meek; was He not meek Whom sinners
    mocked ?
The mourners ? sent not He the Comforter ?
Zeal for the good ; was He not militant ?
The merciful ; He came to bring us mercy ;
The pure in heart ; was He not virgin-born ?
Peacemakers; is not He the Prince of Peace ?
Sufferers for God ; He suffered first for man.
O Virtues blest by Christ, high doctrines ye !
Dread mysteries ; royal records ; standards red
Wrapped by the warrior King, His warfare past,
Around His soldiers' bosoms ! Recognise
O man, that majesty in lowness hid !
Put on Christ's garments. Fools shall call them
    rags—
Heed not their scoff ! A prince's child is man,
Born in the purple ; but his royal robes
None other are than those the Saviour dyed,
Treading His Passion's wine-press all alone :
Of such alone be proud ! '
                      The old man paused ;
Then stretched his arms abroad, and said : 'This
    day
Like eight great Angels making way from Heaven
Each following each, those Eight Beatitudes,
Missioned to earth by Him who made the earth

Have sought you out! What welcome shall be
    theirs?'
In silence long he stood; in silence watched
With faded cheek now flushed and widening eyes
The advance of those high tidings. As a man
Who, when the sluice is cut, with beaming gaze
Pursues the on-rolling flood from fall to fall,
Green branch adown it swept, and showery spray
Silvering the berried copse, so followed Bede
The progress of those high Beatitudes
Brightening with visible beams of faith and love
That host in ampler circles, speechless some
And some in passionate converse. Saddest brows
Most quickly caught, that hour, the glory-touch,
Reflected it the best.

              In such discourse
Peaceful and glad the hours went by, though Bede
Had sought that valley less to preach the Word
Than see once more his children. Evening nigh
He shared their feast; and heard with joy like
    theirs
Their village harp; and smote that harp himself.
In turn become their scholar, hour by hour
Forth dragged he records of their chiefs and kings,
Untangling ravelled evidence, and still
Tracking traditions upward to their source,
Like him, that Halicarnassean sage,

Of antique history sire. 'I trust, my friends,
To leave your sons, for lore by you bestowed
Fair recompense, large measure well pressed down,
Recording still God's kingdom in this land,
History which all may read, and gentle hearts
Loving, may grow in grace. Long centuries
    passed,
If wealth should make this nation's heart too fat,
And things of earth obscure the things of heaven,
Haply such chronicle may prompt high hearts
Wearied with shining nothings, back to cast
Remorseful gaze through mists of time, and note
That rock whence they were hewn. From youth
    to age
Inmate of yonder convent on the Tyne,
I question every pilgrim, priest or prince
Or peasant grey, and glean from each his sheaf :
Likewise the Bishops here and Abbots there
Still send me deed of gift, or chronicle
Or missive from the Apostolic See.
Praise be to God Who fitteth for his place
Not only high but mean ! With wisdom's strength
He filled our mitred Wilfrid, born to rule ;
To saintly Cuthbert gave the spirit of prayer ;
On me, as one late born, He lays a charge
Slender, yet helpful still.'
                            Then spake a man
Burly and big, that last at banquet sat,

P

'Father, is history true?' and Bede replied,
'The man who seeks for Truth like hidden gold,
And shrinks from falsehood as a leper's touch
Shall write true history; not the truth unmixed
With fancies, base or high; not truth entire;
Yet truth beneficent to man below.
One Book there is that errs not: ye this day
Have learned therefrom your Lord's Beatitudes:
That Book contains its histories—like them none
Since written none from standing point so high,
With insight so inspired, such measure just
Of good and ill, such fruit of aid divine.
The slothful spurn that Book; the erroneous
    warp it:
But they who read its page, or hear it read,
Their guide God's Spirit and the Church of God,
Shall hear the voice of Truth for ever nigh,
Shall see the Truth, now sunlike, and anon
Like dagger-point of light from dewy grass
Flashed up, a word that yet confutes a life,
Pierces perchance a nation's heart; shall see
Far more—the Truth Himself in human form
Walking not farms and fields of Eastern lands
Alone, but these our English fields and farms;
Shall see Him on the dusky mount at prayer;
Shall see Him in the street and by the bier;
Shall see Him at the feast and at the grave;
Now from the boat discoursing, and anon

Staying the storm or walking on its waves ;
Thus shall our land become a holy land
And holy those who tread her ! ' Lifting then
Heavenward that tome, he said, ' The Book of
    God !
As stands God's Church 'mid kingdoms of this
    world
Holy alone, so stands 'mid books this Book !
Within the " Upper Chamber " once that Church
Lived in small space ; to-day she fills the
    world :
This Book which seems so slender is a world :
It is an Eden of mankind restored;
It is a heavenly City lit with God :
From it the Spirit and the Bride say " Come : "
Blessed who reads this Book ! '
                                Above the woods
Meantime the stars shone forth ; and came that
    hour
When to the wanderer and the toiling man
Repose is sweet. Upon a leaf-strewn bed
The venerable man slept well that night :
Next morning young and old pursued his steps
As southward he departed. From a hill
O'er-looking far that sea-like forest tract
And many a church far-kenned through smokeless
    air
He blessed that kneeling concourse, adding thus,

'Pray still O friends for me, since spiritual foes
Threat most the priesthood:—pray that holy
    death,
Due warning given, may close a life too blest!
Pray well since I for you have laboured well,
Yea, and will labour till my latest sigh,
Not only seeking you in wilds and woods
Year after year, but in my cell at night
Changing to accents of your native tongue
God's Book Divine. Farewell, my friends, fare-
    well!'
He left them; in his heart this thought, 'How
    like
The great death-parting every parting seems!'
But deathless hopes were with him—and the
    May;
His grief went by.
                    So passed a day of Bede's;
And many a studious year was stored with such;
Enough but one for sample. Two glad weeks
He and his comrade onward roved. At eve
Convent or hamlet known long since and loved
Gladly received them. Bede with heart as glad
Renewed with them the memory of old times,
Recounted benefits by him received
Then strong in youth, from just men passed away,
And preached his Master still with power so sweet
The listeners ne'er forgat him. Evermore,

Parting, he planted in the ground a cross
And bade the neighbours till their church was
  built
Round it to pray. Meanwhile his youthful mate
Changed by degrees. The ever-varying scene,
The biting breath yet balmy breast of Spring,
And most of all that old man's valiant heart
Triumphed above his sadness, fancies gay
Pushing beyond it like those sunnier shoots
That gild the dark vest of the vernal pine.
He took account of all things as they passed;
He laughed; he told his tale. With quiet joy
His friend remarked that change. The second
  week
They passed to Durham; next to Walsingham;
To Gilling then; to stately Richmond soon
High throned above her Ouse; to Ripon last:
Then Bede made pause, and spake; 'Not far is
  York;
Egbert who fills Paulinus' saintly seat
Would see me gladly: such was mine intent,
But something in my bosom whispers "Nay,
Return to that fair river crossed by night
The Tees, the fairest in this Northern land:
Beside its restless wave thine eye shall rest
On vision lovelier far and more benign
Than all it yet hath seen."' Northward once
  more

They faced, and three days travelling reached at eve
Again those ivied cliffs that guard the Tees:
There as they stood a homeward dove with flight
Softer for contrast with that turbulent stream
Sailed through the crimson eve. 'No sight like that!'
Thus murmured Bede; 'ever to me it seems
A Christian soul returning to its rest.'
A shade came o'er his countenance as he mused;
Algar remarked that shade, though what it meant
He knew not yet. The old man from that hour
Seemed mirthful less, less buoyant, beaming less,
Yet not less glad.
    At dead of night, while hung
The sacred stars upon their course half-way
He left his couch, and thus to Egbert wrote
Meek man—too meek—the brother of the king,
With brow low bent and onward sweeping hand
Great words, world-famed: 'Remember thine account!
The Lord's Apostles are the salt o' the earth;
Let salt not lose its savour! Flail and fan
Are given thee. Purge thou well thy threshing floor!
Repel the tyrant; hurl the hireling forth;
That so from thy true priests true hearts may learn
True faith, true love, and nothing but the truth!'

Before the lark he rose the morrow morn
And stood by Algar's bed, and spake : 'Arise !
Playtime is past : the great good work returns ;
To Jarrow speed we !' Homeward, day by day
Thenceforth they sped with foot that lagged no
    more,
That youth, at first so mournful, joyous now,
That old man oft in thought. Next day while
    eve
Descended dim and clung to Hexham's groves
He passed its abbey, silent. Wonder-struck
Algar demanded, 'Father, pass you thus
That church where holy John[1] ordained you
    priest ?
Pass you its Bishop, Acca, long your friend ?
Yearly he woos your visit ; tells you tales
Of Hexham's saintly Wilfrid ; shows you still
Chalice or cross new-won from distant shores :
Nor these alone :—glancing from such last year
A page he read you of some Pagan bard
With smiles ; yet ended with a sigh, and said
" Where is he now ?"' The man of God replied :
' Desire was mine to see mine ancient friend ;
For that cause came I hither :—time runs short ' :—
Then, Algar sighing, thus he added mild,
' Let go that theme ; thy mourning time is past :
Thy gladsome time is now.' As on they walked

[1] St. John of Beverley.

Later he spake : 'It may be I was wrong ;
Old friends should part in hope.'

                               On Jarrow's towers,
Bright as that sunrise while that pair went
    forth
The sunset glittered when, their wanderings past,
Bede and his comrade by the bank of Tyne
Once more approached the gates. Six hundred
    monks
Flocked forth to meet them. 'They had grieved,
    I know,'
Thus spake, low-voiced the venerable man,
'If I had died remote. To spare that grief
Before the time intended I returned.'
Sadly that comrade looked upon his face,
Yet saw there nought of sadness. Silent each
Advanced they till they met that cowlèd host :
But three weeks later on his bed the boy
Remembered well those words.

                              Within a cell
To Algar's near that later night a youth
Wrote thus to one far off, his earliest friend :
'O blessed man ! was e'er a death so sweet !
He sang that verse, "A dreadful thing it is
To fall into the hands of God, All-Just ;"
Yet awe in him seemed swallowed up by love ;
And oft-times with the Prophets and the Psalms

He mixed glad minstrelsies of English speech,
Songs to his childhood dear!

                      'O blessed man!
The Ascension Feast of Christ our Lord drew
    nigh;
He watched that splendour's advent; sang its
    hymn:
"All-Glorious King, Who, triumphing this day
Into the heaven of heavens didst make ascent,
Forsake us not, poor orphans! Send Thy Spirit
The Spirit of Truth the Father's promised Gift
To comfort us, His children : Hallelujah."
And when he reached that word, "Forsake us
    not,"
He wept—not tears of grief. With him we wept;
Alternate wept; alternate read our rite;
Yea, while we wept we read. So passed that day,
The sufferer thanking God with labouring breath,
"God scourges still the son whom He receives."

  'Undaunted, unamazed, daily he wrought
His daily task; instruction daily gave
To us his scholars round him ranged, and said,
"I will not have my pupils learn a lie,
Nor, fruitless, toil therein when I am gone."
Full well he kept an earlier promise, made
Oft-times to humble folk, in English tongue
Rendering the Gospels of the Lord. On these

The last of these, the Gospel of Saint John,
He laboured till the close. The days went by,
And still he toiled, and panted, and gave thanks
To God with hands uplifted ; yea, in sleep
He made thanksgiving still. When Tuesday came
Suffering increased ; he said, "My time is short ;
How short it is I know not." Yet we deemed
He knew the time of his departure well.

 'On Wednesday morn once more he bade us
   write :
We wrote till the third hour, and left him then,
To pace, in reverence of that Feast all-blest,
Our cloister court with hymns. Meantime a youth
Algar by name there was who left him never ;
The same that hour beside him sat and wrote :
More late he questioned : "Father well-beloved,
One chapter yet remaineth ; have you strength
To dictate more ?" He answered : "I have
   strength ;
Make ready son, thy pen, and swiftly write."
When noon had come he turned him round and
   said,
"I have some little gifts for those I love ;
Call in the Brethren ;" adding with a smile
"The rich man makes bequests and why not I ?"
Then gifts he gave, incense or altar-cloth,
To each commanding, "Pray ye for my soul !

Be strong in prayer and offering of the Mass
For ye shall see my face no more on earth :
Blessed hath been my life ; and time it is
That unto God God's creature should return ;
Yea, I desire to die and be with Christ."
Thus speaking he rejoiced till evening's shades
Darkened around us. That disciple young
Once more addressed him, "Still one verse remains ;"
The master answered, "Write and write with speed ;"
And dictated. The young man wrote ; then said
"'Tis finished now." The man of God replied,
"Well say'st thou son, ''tis finished.' In thy hands
Receive my head and move it gently round
For comfort great it is and joy in death
Thus, on this pavement of my little cell
Facing that happy spot whereon so oft
In prayer I knelt, to sit once more in prayer
Thanking my Father." "Glory," then he sang
" To God, the Father, Son, and Holy Ghost ;"
And with that latest Name upon his lips
Passed to the Heavenly Kingdom.'
        Thus with joy
Died holy Bede upon Ascension Day
In Jarrow Convent. May he pray for us
And all who read his annals of God's Church
In England housed, his great bequest to man !

ON VISITING A HAUNT OF COLERIDGE'S.

From Lynton, where the double streams
   Through forest-hung ravines made way,
   And bounded into seas late grey
That shook with morning's earliest beams
   I wandered on to Porlock Bay;

And thence, for love of him who sang
   His happiest songs beside their rills,
   To 'seaward Quantock's heathy hills'[1]
Advanced, while lane and hedge-grove rang,
   And all the song-birds 'had their wills.'

There, like a sweet face dimmed with pain
   The scene grew dark with mist and shower:
   Its yellow leaf the autumnal bower
Moulted full fast; and as the rain
   Washed the last fragrance from the flower

I heard the blue-robed schoolboy's tongue
   Thrilling Christ's Hospital once more
   With mythic chant and antique lore
While round their Bard his playmates hung
   Wondering, and sighed, the witchery o'er.

[1] See Coleridge's 'Recollections of Love.'

I saw him tread soft Devon's coombes—
  Ah! thence he drew that southern grace
  Which in his songs held happy place
Amid their mystic northland glooms,
  Like some strange flower of alien race:

Nor less 'twas his the steeps to climb
  Where, high o'er cloud and precipice,
  Mind, throned among the seas of ice,
Watches from specular tower sublime
  Far vis'o is kenned through freezing skies,

Outlines of Thought, like hills through mist
  That stretch athwart the Infinite
  In dread mathesis lines of light—
Such Thoughts the Muse's spell resist;
  Above her mark they wing their flight!

The songs he gave us, what were they
  But preludes to some loftier rhyme
  That would not leave the spheral chime,
The concords of eternal day,
  And speak itself in words of Time?

O ever-famished Heart! O hands
  That still 'drew nectar in a sieve!'
  At birth of thine what witch had leave
To bind such strength in willow bands,
  The web half-woven to unweave?

O for those Orphic songs unheard
   That lived but in the Singer's thought!
   Who sinned? Whose hand the ruin wrought?
Unworthy was the world or Bard
   To clasp those Splendours all but caught?

What Bard of all who e'er have sung
   Since that lark sang when Eve had birth
   Song's *inmost* soul had uttered forth
Like thee? from Song's asperge had flung
   Her lesser baptism o'er the earth?

The world's base Poets have not kept
   Song's vigil on her vestal height,
   Nor scorned false pride and foul delight,
Nor with the weepers rightly wept,
   Nor seen God's visions in the night!

Profane to enthrone the Sense, and add
   A gleam that lies to shapes that pass,
   Ah me! in song as in a glass
They might have shown us glory-clad
   His Face Who ever is and was!

They might have shown us cloud and leaf
   Lit with the radiance uncreate;
   Love throned o'er vanquished Lust and Hate,
Joy, gem-distilled through rocks of Grief,
   And Justice conquering Time and Fate!

But they immodest brows have crowned
With violated bud and flower :
Courting the high Muse ' par amour '
Upon her suppliants she hath frowned,
And sent them darkness for a dower.

Thy song was pure : thy heart was high :
Thy genius through its strength was chaste :
And if that genius ran to waste
Unblemished as its native sky
O'er diamond rocks the river raced !

Great Bard ! To thee in youth my heart
Rushed as the maiden's to the boy
When love, too blithesome to be coy,
No want forbodes and feels no smart,
A selfless love, self-brimmed with joy !

Still sporting with those amaranth leaves
That shape for few their coronals
I ask not on whose head it falls
That crown the Fame Pandemian weaves—
Thee, thee the Fame Uranian calls !

For wildered feet point thou the path
Which mounts to where triumphant sit
The Assumed of Earth all human yet,
From sun-glare safe and tempest's wrath,
Who sing for love ; nor those forget

The Elders crowned that, singing, fling
  Their crowns upon the Temple floor ;
  Those Elders ever young, though hoar,
Who count all praise an idle thing
Save His who lives for evermore !

THE DEATH OF COPERNICUS.

COPERNICUS died at Fraemberg, a small city at the mouth of the Vistula, A.D. 1543, and, as has been said, though the fact is not certain, the day after he received the first printed copy of that great work, dedicated to Pope Paul III., which embodied his astronomical discoveries, and substituted the Copernican for the Ptolemaic system of the universe. That work he had withheld from publication for thirty-six years, fearing lest the conclusions he had arrived at might possibly prove unsound scientifically, and, *in that case*, till confuted, be dangerous to Faith. These misgivings he had discarded on re-examining the grounds of his philosophy.

HAIL, silent, chaste, and ever sacred stars !
Ye bind my life in one ! I well remember
When first your glory pierced my youthful heart :
'Twas Christmas Eve near midnight. From a boat
I watched you long ; then, rowing, faced the deep :
Above the storm-loved cliff of Elsinore
Sworded Orion high and higher rose
With brightening belt. The city clocks struck twelve :
Straight from the countless towers rang out their chimes

Hailing the Babe new-born. Along the sea
Vibration waved ; and in its depth the stars
Danced as they flashed answering that rapturous
    hymn
'Glory to God on high and peace on earth.'
I shall not long behold them saith my leech :
He errs : I suffer little.

                On my bed
Yon lies my tome—one man's bequest to men.
Is the gift good ? From youth to age I toiled
A gleaner in the starry harvest field :
Lo, there one gathered sheaf—
I think I laboured with a stainless aim
If not a single aim. In ancient times
Pythagoras had gleams of this high lore :
Let coming ages stamp his name upon it ;
I count it his, not mine.

                    My earlier book
In substance was as this. But thus I mused ;
Christ's simple ones may take offence and cry
' 'Tis written, "God hath made the earth so
    strong
That it cannot be moved ;" science avers
It moves around the sun.' Such questioner
Deserves all reverence. Faith is more than
    Science ;
But 'twixt the interpretation and the text

Lies space world-wide. That text meant this—no
    more—
So solid is the earth concussion none,
Though mountains fell, can move it. Here is
    naught
Of motion round the sun. Solidity
To such advance were needful not a bar :
Far flies the pebble forward flung; the flower
Drops at the flinger's foot.
                      Again I mused ;
The Truth of Nature with the Truth Revealed
Accords perforce ; not so the illusive gloss
By Nature's scholiasts forced on Nature's page :
That gloss of Ptolemy's made great Nature lie
A thousand years, and more. Through countless
    errors
Thus only, Science feels her way to Truth.
May I not err like Ptolemy ? Distrustful
I hid my book for thirty years and six
Cross-questioning with fresh inquest patient skies
And found there nothing that arraigned my lore,
Much that confirmed it. From the Minster tower
Canon that time at Warnia though unworthy,
I made me charts of angle, sine, and arc :
Those vigils left my feet so numbed at morn
They scarce could find the altar-step, my hands
Scarce lift the chalice ! Day by day I prayed
With adjuration added, 'If, my God,

THE DEATH OF COPERNICUS.

Thou seest my pride suborn my faculties
Place me, a witless one, among those witless
That beg beneath church porches.' Likewise I
   sued
The poor beside whose beds I ministered—
For their sake I had learned the healing craft—
To fence me with their prayers.

       Discovered truths
I blabbed not to the many but the wise,
Such men as raised our stateliest fanes. In these
I found amazement less than I presaged :
There seemed a leaning in the minds of men
As when a leaning cornfield shows the wind
To such results as in Bologna's schools
Made way when there I dwelt. I note this day
The ecclesiastics of the higher sort
Are with me more than those whose lore is Nature ;
These hate the foot that spurns prescription's fence;
Not so my friend the bishop of old Kulm ;
He cries, ' Go forward !' Thirty years ago
Milan's famed painter— he of the ' Last Supper '—
Whispered me thus, 'The earth goes round the
   sun.'
There are whose guess is prophecy.
          This night
I make election : twofold choice is mine ;
The first, to hurl this book on yonder sea ;

The last, to fling it on a flood more vast
And fluctuating more, the mind of man,
Crying, 'Fare forth and take what God shall send!'
One doubt alone remains; no text it touches
But dangers from within.   In days gone by
I saw a youth beside a casement stand
The sea not distant and a heaven all stars:
Christ's Advent was our theme.   He cried, 'Look forth!
Yon skies confute the old Faith! When Earth was young
Wistful as lovers, credulous as children,
Men deemed that Earth the centre of the world
The stars its lackeys and its torch-bearers.
Such science is foredoomed: mankind will learn
This sphere is not God's ocean but one drop
Showered from its spray.   Came God from heaven for that?
Speak no more words!'
                      That was a tragedy!
A mood may pass; yet moods have murdered souls:
It proved not thus with him.
                            I looked again:
That face was as an angel's: from his brow
The cloud had passed.   Reverent, I spake no word:
It may be that my silence helped him best:
Later, albeit at times such moods recurred,

That man was helpful to a nation's soul :
In death he held the Faith.
                      This Earth too small
For Love Divine ! Is God not Infinite ?
If so, His Love is infinite. Too small !
One famished babe meets pity oft from man
More than an army slain ! Too small for Love !
Was Earth too small to be of God created ?
Why then too small to be redeemed ?
                                The sense
Sees greatness only in the sensuous greatness :
Science in that sees little : Faith sees naught :
The small, the vast, are tricks of earthly vision :
To God, that Omnipresent All-in-Each,
Nothing is small, is far.
                    More late I knew
A hoary man dim-eyed, with restless hands,
A zealot barbed with jibe and scoff still launched
At priests, and kings, and holy womanhood :
One night descending from my tower he spake ;
'A God, and God incarnate but for man
That reasoning beast ; and all yon glittering orbs
In cold obstruction left !'
                      Diverse those twain !
That youth, though dazzled by the starry vastness
And thus despising earth, had awe for God :
That grey-haired fool believed in matter only.
Compassion for those starry races robbed

By earth, like Esau, of their birthright just
Is pretext. They that know not of a God
How know they that the stars have habitants?
'Tis Faith and Hope that spread delighted hands
To such belief; no formal proof attests it.
Concede them peopled ; can the sophist prove
Their habitants are fallen ? That too admitted
Who told him that redeeming foot divine
Ne'er trod those spheres? That fresh assumption
    granted
What then ? Is not the Universe a whole?
Doth not the sunbeam herald from the sun
Gladden the violet's bosom ? Moons uplift
The tides : remotest stars lead home the lost :
Judæa was one country, one alone :
Not less Who died there died for all. The Cross
Brought help to vanished nations : Time opposed
No bar to Love : why then should Space oppose
    one ?
We know not what Time is nor what is Space ;—
Why dream that bonds like theirs constrain the
    Unbounded ?
If Earth be small, likelier it seems that Love
Compassionate most and condescending most .
To Sorrow's nadir depths, should choose that Earth
For Love's chief triumph missioning thence her
    gift
Even to the utmost zenith!

To the Soul
Far more than to the intellect of man
I deemed the gift vouchsafed when on me first
This new-born Science dawned. I said 'Long since
We call God *infinite :* what means that term ?
A boy since childhood walled in one small field
Could answer nothing. He who looks on skies
Ablaze with stars, not hand-maids poor of earth
But known for worlds of measureless bulk and swiftness,
Has mounted to another grade of spirit,
Proceeded man. The stars do this for man ;
They make Infinitude *imaginable :*
God, by our instincts felt as infinite,
When known becomes such to our total being
Mind, spirit, heart, and soul. The greater Theist
Should make the greater Christian.
                              Yet, 'tis true
Best gifts may come too soon. No marvel this :
The earth was shaped for myriad forms of greatness,
As Freedom, Genius, Beauty, Science, Art,
Some extant, some to be: such forms of greatness
Are through God's will greatness conditional :
Where Christ is greatest these are great; elsewhere
Great only to betray. Sweetly and sagely

In order grave the Maker of all worlds
Still modulates the rhythm of human progress;
His angels on whose song the seasons float
Keep measured cadence: all good things keep time
Lest Good should strangle Better. Aristotle
Aspired like me to base on fact and proof
Nature's philosophy. Fate said him nay:
That Fate was kindness hidden—
The natural science of great Aristotle
Died young: his logic lived and helped the Church
To map her Christian Science.
                        Ancient Thought
And Christian Faith, opposed in most beside,
Held man in reverence, each. Much came of that:
Matter dethroned, a place remained for spirit:
Old Grecian song called man creation's Lord;
The Christian Creed named him his Maker's Image.;
One was a humble reverence; one a proud:
Science that day perchance had made men prouder;
The Ptolemaic scheme had place and use
Till Christian Faith conquering the earth had crowned it:
The arch complete its centering is removed:
That Faith which franchised first the soul of man
Franchises next his mind.

Another knowledge
Man's appanage now, was snatched awhile from
  men,
The lore of antique ages said or sung:
It rolled, a river through the Athenian vales;
It sank as though by miracle in earth:
A fount unsealed by hand divine, it leaps
Once more against the sun.
                         That strange new birth
Had place when first I trod Italian soil:
Men spake of bards to Dante's self unknown
To Francis, Bernard, Dominic, Aquinas:
Great Albert knew them not! The oracles
Of lying gods were dumb: but dumb not less
The sage Greek poets, annalists, orators,
For God had uttered voice, and leaned from
  heaven
Waiting the earth's response. The air was mute,
Mute, for the Saviour God had breathed it late,
Left it His latest sigh. The ages passed:
Alone were Apostolic voices heard;
Then Fathers of the Church; the Schoolmen
  last.
Clamour had ceased: the "Credo" for that cause
Was plainlier heard. The winds and waves had
  fallen;
And there was a great calm—stillness of spirit
At heart of storm extern. At last God's Truth

Had built o'er earth the kingdom of God's Peace:
The penance-time was passed: Greece spake once
    more:
What was that speech but prophecy fulfilled,
'The heathen shall become thy heritage?
The utmost parts of the earth be thy possession?'
Cephisus and Ilyssus flow again:
Grey wastes with roses flame. Two epochs blend;
Shall not God's angels reap two harvest fields
Severing the wheat from tares?
                      Severance is needful;
Yea, needfuller yet will prove as ages pass:
The nobler songs of Greece divulged in verse
Such Truths as Nature had retained though
    fallen,
Man's heart had prized. Aye, but with these
    there mixed
Music debasing. Christendom this day
Confronts two gifts and trials likewise twain:
She must become the mother of great Nations;
Each Nation with the years will *breed* its Book,
Its Bible uninspired. But if these Books
Should prove but sorcerers' juggling wares, these
    prophets
Stand up false prophets and their word a lie,
A voice from those two Books of Greece and Rome
Will sound their sentence, crying; 'In the night
We sang sweet songs the auguries of dawn;

We sang the Mother-land, the household loves,
The all-reverend eld, the virgin sanctitude,
The stranger's right, the altar reared to Pity;
Ye, 'mid the noontide glories turned to black,
Outshamed our worst with worse.'
                              Should that voice peal
Woe to the Nations which have sinned that sin!
Truth's golden bowl will at the cistern break,
Song's daughters be brought low.
                              For these two gifts,
The Science new, the Old Lore revived, the time
Seems opportune alike. The earth finds rest :
That Rome which warred on Christ is judged;
    has vanished;
Those direful heresies of three centuries more,
The hordes barbaric, and, barbaric thrice
Those Christian Emperors vexing still Christ's
    Church :—
The Antipopes are gone, not less : the Impostor
Scowls at the West in vain. Yet who can tell
If in some age remote or near a cloud
Blacker than aught that shook the olden world
May rush not from clear skies? That hour
    upon us
"*Quieta non movere*" may become
Wisdom's sum total; to repress, not spur
Progressive thought the hour's necessity;
Against their will the truthfullest spirits may cry

'Better to wait than launch the bark of knowledge
There when the breakers roar!
                    The time is fit:—
Work, and in hope, though sin that hope may
    cheat;
Work, knowing this, that when God's lesser gifts
Are mocked by mortals, God into that urn
Which stands for aye gift-laden by His throne
Thrusts deeplier yet His hand and upward draws
His last—then chief—of mercies—Retribution.
Should man abusing use this knowledge vast
Not for relieving of God's suffering poor
But doubling of their burthens; not for peace
But keener sharpening of war's battle-axe
And fleshlier solace of the idle and rich,
God will to such redouble pain for sin.
Such lot may lie before us. This is sure
That, as colossal Sanctity walks oft
In humblest vales, not less a pigmy race
May strut on mountains. If from heights of
    science
Men should look forth o'er worlds on worlds
    unguessed
And find therein no witness to their God,
Nought but man's image chaunting hymns to man
'Great is thy wisdom, Man, and strong thy hand,'
God will repay the madness of that boast
With madness guilty less, a brain imbecile.

Races there live, once sage and brave, that now
Know not to light a fire ! If impious men
Press round Truth's gate with Intellect's fleshlier
    lust—
For what is Godless Intellect but fleshly ?—
Sudden a glacial wind shall issue forth
And strike those vile ones blind !
                            Should that day come
Let no man cease from hope. Intensest ill
Breeds good intensest. For the sons of God
That knowledge won by bad men will survive.
If fleets one day should pass the onrushing storm
That Cross which lights their prow will reach but
    sooner
The lands that sit in night. If Empires new
Wage war on Faith, each drop of martyr blood
Will sow once more Faith's harvest. Virgin
    spirits
Raised from a child-like to an angel pureness
Will walk in Chastity's sublimer flame,
Households become as convents grave and high,
God's earthquake shake men to their fitting places
True men and false, the sons of light and night,
No more as now confused. God's Church will
    make,
Since though she errs not yet her best may err,
For sins of good men dead due expiation,
Then for her second triumph claim as site

A planet's not an empire's girth. True kings
Will fence their thrones with freemen not with
    serfs ;
True priests by serving rule. The Tree of Life
First made our spirits food, that Tree which
    slew us
Will prove her sister. Knowledge *then* will clasp
Supremacy o'er matter, earth's fruition
Not by the facile plucking of a fruit
But by the valorous exercise austere
Of faculties, God's gift.
                    'Lift up your heads,
Ye everlasting gates,' the Psalmist sang
'So shall the King of Glory enter in.'
Lives there who doubts that when the starry gates
Lift up their heads like minster porches vast
At feasts before a marvelling nation's eyes,
And show, beyond, the universe of God,
Lives there who doubts that, entering there, man's
    mind
Must see before it far a God Who enters
Flashing from star to star? Lives there who
    doubts
That those new heavens beyond all hope distent
Must sound their Maker's praise? Religion's self
That day shall wear an ampler crown. All Truths
Now constellated in the Church's Creed
Yet dim this day because man's mind is dim,

Perforce dilating as man's mind dilates
O'er us must hang, a new Theology,
Our own, yet nobler even as midnight heavens
Through crystal ether kenned more sharply shine
Than when mist veiled the stars! Let others
    doubt—
My choice is made.

    The stars! Once more they greet me!
Thanks to the wind that blows yon casement back!
'Tis cold : but vigils old have taught me patience.
Is this the last time, O ye stars? Not so;
'Tis not the death-chill yet. Those northern
    heavens
Yield me once more that Northern Sign long
    loved,
That northern sea, its glass, though many a star
Faints now in broader beams. Yon winter moon
Has changed this cell thick-walled and oft-times
    dim
Into a silver tent. O light, light, light,
How great thou art! Thou only, free of space,
Bindest the universe of God in one :
Matter, methinks, in thee is turned to spirit :
What if our bodies, death-subdued, shall rise
All light—compact of light!
      I had forgotten
Good Cardinal Schomberg's missive: here it lies :

I read it three weeks past. 'The Holy Father
Wills that your labours stand divulged to man;
Wills likewise that his name should grace your
    tome
As dedicate to him.' I read in haste:
That such high grace should 'scape my memory
    thus
Argues, I think, some failure of my powers.
So be it! Their task is wrought.
                          The tide descends:
The caves send forth anew those hoarse sea-
    thunders
Lulled when full-flood satiates their echoing roofs:
They tell me this, that God, their God, hath
    spoken
And the great deep obeys. That deep forsakes
The happy coasts where fishers spread their nets,
The fair green slopes with snowy flocks bespread,
The hamlets red each morn with cloaks of girls
And loud with shouting children. Forth he fares
To solitudes of ocean waste and wide
Cheered by that light he loves. I too obey:
I too am called to face the Infinite,
Leaving familiar things and faces dear
Of friends and tomes forth leaning from yon wall:
Me too the Uncreated Light shall greet
When cleansed to bear it. O, how sweet was
    life!

How sweeter must have proved had I been
    worthy—
Grant me Thy Beatific Vision, Lord :
Then shall these eyes star-wearied see and live !
1889.

AUTUMNAL ODE.
DEDICATED TO MY SISTER.

I.

MINSTREL and Genius to whose songs or sighs
  The round earth modulates her changeful sphere,
That bend'st in shadow from yon western skies
  And lean'st, cloud-hid, along the woodlands sere,
  Too deep thy notes, too pure, for mortal ear !
    Yet Nature hears them : without aid of thine
    How sad were her decline !
From thee she learns with just and soft gradation
  Her dying hues in death to harmonise ;
  Through thee her obsequies
A glory wear that conquers desolation.
Through thee she singeth, 'Faithless were the sighing
  Breathed o'er a beauty only born to fleet :
A holy thing and precious is the dying
  Of that whose life was innocent and sweet.
    From many a dim retreat

Lodged on high-bosomed, echoing mountain lawn
Or chiming convent 'mid dark vale withdrawn,
From cloudy shrine or rapt oracular seat
Voices of loftier worlds that saintly strain repeat.

II.

It is the Autumnal Epode of the year :
   The Nymphs that urge the seasons on their round
They to whose green lap flies the startled deer
   When bays the far-off hound,
They that drag April by the rain-bright hair,
Though sun-showers daze her and the rude winds scare,
   O'er March's frosty bound,
They by whose warm and furtive hand unwound
   The cestus falls from May's new-wedded breast—
Silent they stand beside dead Summer's bier
   With folded palms and faces to the West,
And their loose tresses sweep the dewy ground.

III.

A sacred stillness hangs upon the air,
   A sacred clearness. Shapes remote draw nigh :
Glistens yon Elm-grove to its heart laid bare
   And all articulate in its symmetry
   With here and there a branch that from on high

Far flashes washed in wan and watery gleam :
Beyond, the glossy lake lies calm—a beam
Upheaved, as if in sleep, from its slow central
    stream.

IV.

This quiet—is it Truth, or some fair mask ?
    Is pain no more ?   Shall Sleep be lord, not
        Death ? .
Shall sickness cease to afflict and overtask
    The spent and labouring breath ?
Is there 'mid all yon farms and fields, this day,
    No grey old head that drops ? No darkening
        eye ?
Spirits of Pity, lift your hands and pray—
    Each hour, alas, men die !

V.

The love songs of the Blackbird now are done :
    Upon the o'ergrown, loose, red-berried cover
The latest of late warblers sings as one
    That trolls at random when the feast is over :
        From bush to bush the dusk-bright cobwebs
            hover
        Silvering the dried-up rill's exhausted urn ;
No breeze is fluting o'er the green morass ;
Nor falls the thistle-down : in deep-drenched grass
        Now blue, now red, the shifting dew-gems
            burn.

VI.

Mine ear thus torpid held, methinks mine eye
  Is armed the more with visionary power:
  As with a magnet's force each redd'ning bower
Compels me through the woodland pageantry:
Slowly I track the forest skirt: emerging,
  Slowly I climb from pastoral steep to steep:
I see far mists from reedy valleys surging:
  I follow the procession of white sheep
    That fringe with wool old stock and ruined rath,
How staid to-day, how eager when the lambs
    Went leaping round their dams!
I cross the leaf-choked stream from stone to stone,
  Pass the hoar ash tree, trace the upland path,
The furze-brake that in March all golden shone
  Reflected in the shy kingfisher's bath.

VII.

No more from full-leaved woods that music
    swells
  Which all the summer filled the satiate ear:
A fostering sweetness still from bosky dells
  Murmurs; but I can hear
A harsher sound when down, at intervals,
The dry leaf rattling falls.
Dark as those spots which herald swift disease
The death-blot marks for death the leaf yet firm:
Beside the leaf down-trodden trails the worm:

In forest depths the haggard, whitening grass
Repines at youth departed. Half-stripped trees
   Reveal, as one who says, 'Thou too must pass,'
Plainlier each day their quaint anatomies.
Yon Poplar grove is troubled! Bright and bold
Babbled his cold leaves in the July breeze
As though above our heads a runnel rolled:
   His mirth is o'er; subdued by old October
     He counts his lessening wealth, and, sadly sober,
Tinkles his minute tablets of wan gold.

VIII.

Be still, ye sighs of the expiring year!
   A sword there is: ye play but with the sheath!
Whispers there are more piercing yet more dear
     Than yours, that come to me the boughs beneath;
And well-remembered footsteps known of old
   Tread soft the mildewed mould.
O magic memory of the things that were;
   Of those whose hands our childish locks carest,
Of one so angel-like in tender care,
   Of one in majesty so god-like drest;
O phantom faces painted on the air
   Of friend or sudden guest;—
I plead in vain:
The woods revere but cannot heal my pain.

Ye sheddings from the Yew tree and the Pine
  If on your rich and aromatic dust
    I laid my forehead, and my hands put forth
In that last beam which warms the forest floor
No answer to my yearnings would be mine;
To me no answer through those branches hoar
  Would reach in noonday trance or moony gust!
    Her secret Heaven would keep, and mother Earth
Speak from her deep heart, 'Where thou know'st not, trust!'

IX.

That pang is past. Once more my pulses keep
  A tenor calm that knows nor grief nor joy;
Once more I move as one that died in sleep
  And treads, a Spirit, the haunts he trod, a boy,
And sees them like-unlike, and sees beyond:
Then earthly life comes back, and I despond.
Ah life, not life! Dim woods of crimsoned beech
  That swathe the hills in sacerdotal stoles
Burn on, burn on! the year ere long will reach
  That day made holy to Departed Souls,
The day whereon man's heart, itself a priest,
  Descending to that Empire pale wherein
  Beauty and Sorrow dwell, but pure from Sin,
Holds with God's Church at once its fast and feast.

Dim woods, they, they alone your vaults should
    tread,
  The sad and saintly Dead !
Your pathos those alone ungrieved could meet
  Who fit them for the Beatific Vision:
The things which, as they pass us, seem to cheat
  To them would be a music-winged fruition,
  A cadence sweetest in its soft subsiding ;
  Transience to them were dear ; for theirs the
    abiding—
Dear as that Pain which clears from fleshly film
  The spirit's eye, matures each spirit-germ
  Frost-bound on earth, but at the appointed term
Mirror of Godhead in the immortal realm.

X.

Lo there the regal Exiles !—under shades
  Deeper than ours, yet in a finer air—
Climbing, successive, elders, youths, and maids,
  The penitential mountain's ebon stair :
  The earth-shadow clips that halo round their
    hair :
And as lone outcasts watch a moon that wanes
Receding slowly o'er their native plains,
  Thus watch they wistful something far but fair.
    Serene they stand, and wait
    Self-banished by the ever-open gate ;

Awhile self-banished from the All-pitying Eyes,
Lest mortal stain should blot their Paradise.
Silent they pace, ascending high and higher
   The hills of God, a hand on every heart
That willing burns, a vase of cleansing fire
   Fed by God's love in souls from God apart:
Each lifted face with thirst of long desire
   Is pale; but o'er it grows a mystic sheen
   Because on them God's Face—by them unseen—
Is turned, through narrowing darkness, hourly nigher.

XL

Sad thoughts, why roam ye thus in your unrest
   The bourne unseen? Why scorn our mortal bound?
Is it not kindly, Earth's maternal breast?
   Is it not fair, her head with vine-wreaths crowned?
Farm-yard and barn are heaped with golden store;
   High piled the sheaves illume the russet plain;
Hedges and hedge-row trees are yellowed o'er
   With waifs and trophies of the labouring wain:
Why murmur, 'Change is change when downward ranging;
Spring's upward change but pointed to the unchanging?'

Yet, Oh how just your sorrow, if ye knew
　　The true grief's sanction true !
'Tis not the flight of youth that chiefly moves
　　us ;
　'Tis not alone the pang for friends departed :
The Autumnal pain that raises while it proves us
　　Wells from a holier source and deeper-hearted !
For this a sadness swells above our mirth ;
　For this a bitter runs beneath the sweetness;
　　The throne that shakes not is the Spirit's
　　　right ;
　　The heart and hope of Man are infinite ;
Heaven is his home, and, exiled here on earth,
　　Completion most betrays the incompleteness !

XII.

Heaven is his home.—But hark ! the breeze
　　increases
　The sunset forests, catching sudden fire
　　Flash, swell, and sing, a million-organed choir:
Roofing the West, rich clouds in glittering fleeces
　　O'er-arch ethereal spaces and divine
　　Of heaven's clear hyaline.
No dream is this ! Beyond that radiance golden
　God's Sons I see, His armies bright and strong ;
The ensanguined Martyrs here with palms high
　　holden,
　The virgins there, a lily-lifting throng !

The Splendours nearer draw. In choral blending
    The Prophets' and the Apostles' chant I hear;
I see the Salem of the Just descending
    With gates of pearl and diamond bastions sheer.
The walls are agate and chalcedony:
    On jacinth street and jasper parapet
The unwaning light is light of Deity
    Not beam of lessening moon or suns that set.
That indeciduous forestry of spires
    Lets fall no leaf! those lights can never range:
Saintly fruitions and divine desires
    Are blended there in rapture without change.
Man was not made for things that leave us,
    For that which goeth and returneth,
For hopes that lift us yet deceive us,
    For love that wears a smile yet mourneth;
Not for fresh forests from the dead leaves springing,
    The cyclic re-creation which, at best,
Yields us—betrayal still to promise clinging—
    But tremulous shadows of the realm of rest:
    For things immortal Man was made,
God's Image latest from His hand,
    Co-heir with Him Who in Man's flesh arrayed
Holds o'er the worlds the Heavenly-Human wand:

His portion this—sublime
To stand where access none hath Space or Time,
Above the starry host, the Cherub band,
To stand—to advance—and, after all, to stand!

Curragh Chase, October, 1876.

www.ingramcontent.com/pod-product-compliance
Lightning Source LLC
Chambersburg PA
CBHW032117230426
43672CB00009B/1770